GEO'S GEMS

ALSO BY

GEO DERICE

The Thirst Is Real

GEO'S GEMS

52 Motivational Gems To Making Your Life A Masterpiece

GEO DERICE

Disclaimer:

In this book you will see references to God as well as the Bible. It is not my intention to impose my beliefs onto you. I respect who and what you believe in and feel free to substitute who and what you believe in when those references are made.

If you would like to purchase bulk copies of *Geo's Gems* contact us at geo@geospeaks.com for discount pricing.

1st edition, July 2020

ISBN-13: 978-0-578-71649-7

Printed in the United States of America

This book is dedicated to all the people who have dreams that they want to see come to pass. Long before they appear as things in the light, they are our thoughts in the dark. This book is a bridge connecting where you are now to where you want to be.

Contents

CONCLUSION

ACKNOWLEDGEMENTS

ABOUT THE AUTHOR

INTRODUCTION

Never in a million years!

I'm so excited about the book you are holding in your hands right now. This is book number two for me (first one - *The Thirst Is Real*). If someone told me years ago that I would ever write a book, I would say, "Never In A Million Years." But, here I am now doing the "never" for a second time. Perhaps my "never" is now becoming an always. It's a crazy when you think about it.

Let me ask you a question, and yes, we are not wasting anytime with this book. It is get-up-in-your-business time. What is your "never in a million years" look like? When your mind wanders and drifts into an abyss, what images come up? What beliefs come up regarding what could be and should be? What things come up that hold you back from being able to fully engage into those thoughts, preventing you from making them things you see with your very own eyes?

This book is designed to help you along that journey of turning things hoped for into things **SEEN.**

Our thoughts are where it starts. There is a saying about how long before something is a thing, it's a thought. Think about anything you've ever seen before. The iPhone, Uber, Airbnb, an airplane, an air fryer (I just had breakfast before writing this), all of the THINGS were once THOUGHTS in someone's mind. The gems in this book are my way of helping you get the things you want the most by helping to shape your thoughts.

I'll be honest, the gems themselves are not magical. By no means is this some hocus pocus kind of stuff. However, these are seeds that when watered can produce some magnificent trees which will produce tons of fruits for you to eat and share with others.

So before we get started, I'd like to share with you how to make the best use of the gems you are about to read. Number one, there are 52 gems in this book, one essentially for every week of the year. The best way to really see these gems work in your life is to tackle them week by week. You will be tempted because they are so good to apply them all right away, but that would be like hanging a picture on a nail that was only hammered once into the wall; it won't stick. Take each gem and really dive deeply into how you can make this your guide for the week. Each day, ask the question of how can I make this gem real to me today?

Number two, don't keep your experiences or engagements with the gems to yourself. As one of the gems shared in this book says, wisdom is never meant to be kept; it is meant to be shared. By sharing these gems and the impact they have on you, you will begin to help others experience the same enlightenment. This helps you in two ways. First way, you get to help others by sharing the gem, but more so, you will not feel comfortable sharing them if you are not applying them, right? So knowing you will share the gems can help you in applying them. Secondly, when you share the gems and the people apply them, you will help to transform the company around you; thus, elevating your own company (you'll see this gem later).

Before we get on the bus and depart on this journey let me give you a final warning: Think of this as me being your flight attendant before takeoff. These gems on the surface will seem simple and your mind might have you say, "I already know that." But do not stop there. Knowing something and understanding it from practice are two different things. Do yourself and me a favor and suspend the disbelief. Give these gems a shot. Give them a chance to do the renewing of your mind that it can do. Thoughts shape the lives we live, so be sponge-like. Be like clay and let these gems mold you into the masterpiece you know deep down you can and should be. Let nothing, and I mean nothing, stop you from experiencing that. One of the greatest tragedies that can happen is you being anything less than your best. If you are ready to turn to the next page, then I know you are ready to dive into these gems. It's time to start the road toward your "never in a million years" moment. Let's put on our seat belts and get ready to go!

GEM #1

Intentions Don't Change Anything. Intentional Actions Do.

INTENTIONS DON'T CHANGE ANYTHING. Intentional actions do. Do you know someone who says they are going to do, but when it came time to do, they did not do? That's a lot of DOs there, but you get the point. Many people plan on doing stuff, and I know we must have plans, but it's important that we understand plans are only part of the equation. The other part of the equation is working the plan. Our intentions—a.k.a. plans, a.k.a. our thoughts—don't become things until we activate them with action.

The BEST INTENTIONS in the world, as great as they are, means nothing if it's not supported with action. The manifestation of our lives relies on action coming along for the ride with our intentions. Intentions are easy. Anyone can have them, The actions are what separates those who live in the "hoped for" stage and those who live in the "my eyes have seen" stage.

It's like those air hand dryers in the airport. The machine has every intention and all the capabilities in the world to dry your hands, but until you activate it by putting your hands under it, nothing happens. Intention alone won't change a life. Intentional action, however, won't stop a life from changing. It's that extra "**umph**" that is needed to see **tri-umph** in your life.

With that being said, what intentions do you have stored up that could use a little action today? Now is as good a time as ever to take your greatness out of the attic and show the world what you are made of.

What you have, the world desperately needs. And while the intent or potential is great, we need to see it.

Your pondering thought for this week, if you do choose to apply this gem, is to simply ask what intentions you have that needs action in order for it to manifest in your life and the lives of those around you.

GEM #2

All Changes Aren't Bad
(Give Yourself Permission To
Change Your Mind)

HAVE YOU EVER FOUND yourself in a situation where
you made a decision and had the urge to change your
mind, but you don't because you don't want the thought
of "I made the wrong decision initially" to register?
Or maybe you're one of those people that has made a
commitment to something and have been trained to
make your yes, your yes, and your no, your no?

In the book *Influence* by Robert Cialdini, he talks about
one method that makes change difficult. This idea is called,
"Commitment and Consistency." Commitment and Consistency are high values that culture has taught us which

is a good thing unless it actually becomes bad without us noticing. For many, this may show up in what your favorite color is. Think back to when you were younger and were asked what your favorite color was, or your favorite food, or your favorite television show. What would it look like if you were all of the sudden to change course and say that is not your favorite color anymore, not your favorite television show anymore? "Commitment and Consistency" tells us that what you said back then is what you need to say now, but it does not take into account what I've learned and hope to share with you here. You ARE NOT where you've been. "Commitment and Consistency" makes sense if you are exactly the same, but it does not apply when over time you've experienced different things and now think differently than you did before.

Too many times people get into relationships with this same idea of commitment and consistency and therefore stay in relationships that started out great, but soon began to tear them apart. What's one to do in that situation? Be loyal and stay? Above all else you need to be loyal to your future self. Your future self has no control over what you are doing and will be a byproduct of what you do right now. If you do what you are doing now and change nothing, will it turn out good for your future self?

This is why this gem is so relevant because I'm on a mission to declare that changing your mind is not a bad thing, sometimes it's for the BETTER. You should be okay with an upgrade, you should be okay wanting more, you should be okay with experiencing new levels in life. The Bible reminds us that God's mercies is new every morning. That does not make the mercy of yesterday bad, it just means that today you get a fresh batch of mercy. I look at change like a dirty diaper. Would you want to be committed and consistent with having a dirty diaper? Of course not. Now I'm not here telling you to be a chronic changer. What I am saying is to break the shackles off when you find yourself in a situation that does not serve you.

All change isn't bad, some is good, so what change have you been reluctant to make because you did not want to seem disloyal? What change have you been reluctant to make because you wanted commitment and consistency to be a high ranking value in spite of how it might be killing you and decreasing your lifespan while stealing all your peace and joy?

Allow this gem to be your permission to evaluate the things in your life and change courses if your future self will benefit from the decision to do so. You are free to do so and let no one or no thing keep you in bondage of your past decisions that aren't serving you. My good friend Christopher Browne tells his students this all the time when decision time comes, "You have to weigh and measure." I suggest you do the same, weigh and measure the cost of changing your mind, don't just assume it's too costly or bad.

GEM #3

Your Company Will Affect Your COMPANY (You're A CEO)

YOUR COMPANY WILL AFFECT your company. You are a CEO! There I said it. You are a BOSS, the Chief Executive Operator of your life, or as we know it, the CO-CEO, since God is the boss of us, right? All joking aside, we know that very few things affect the trajectory of our lives like the people that we surround ourselves with. We've all heard the sayings that you are the sum of the five people you hang around the most or birds of a feather flock together. I remember when T-Mobile used to have the my faves five—do you remember that, where you would be able to call your five people unlimited? Even now, your iPhone still has a favorites section where you can compile your favorite people and get to their number easily. (SN: Am I in your favorites? I'm only kidding.)

It's super important that you realize how important the decision of the company you keep is on your business, a.k.a. life. Have you ever been around people who are just negative? When it's sunny it's too hot, when there is no sun it's too cold, no matter what side of the bed they wake up on, it's always cold? Do you have someone like that in your circle? How does it feel when you are around them too long? What ends up happening to you? You become negative yourself. We just cannot help ourselves.

In the same token, think of anyone you know that is super successful and what do you notice about their surroundings? What kind of company do they have?

When I think of Sean Combs—P Diddy, Love, whatever name he goes by these days—I see YouTube videos with him keeping good company. In fact, there was a video recently of him speaking with Ray Dalio, the best-selling author of the book *Principles*. Is it a surprise that they are both in the company of each other? Absolutely not. It's the same as Jay-Z being in the same room as Warren Buffet; it's all about the company they keep.

There's nothing, **NOTHING,** like the company you keep.

Here are a few questions I want you to ponder with regards to this gem:

What does your company reveal about you?

Is it positive? Is it negative? Are you thriving or surviving? Is your company dying? Are you around those who are doing things, or are you around those who are full of intentions, but are running low on action?

Now is the time to consider who you surround yourself with intentionally and who needs to get cut-off. I know this is cut-throat for many, but listen, your company is on the line. Laying off people isn't easy, but the business of you has to go on, even if that means people have to go on, too.

Here's a bonus tip by the way: Some company does not have to be physical to have a positive impact. Sometimes the best company comes from the books you surround yourself with. Some of the company that I keep, I've never met before. I've never met Andy Stanley, but he's part of the company that I keep. I've never met or sat down with a Kevin Hart, but his book is in my company. I have lists upon lists and you should, too. Be intentional about the company you keep, as if your life depends on it, because it does.

GEM #4

Put In Extra Work For Those Rainy Days

I WAS HAVING A conversation with a fri-ent (friend + client) and she told me about a health condition that is tied to the weather which impacts how we feel. It's called seasonal affective disorder. After sharing this with me, it provided great context to the "content" I was experiencing when it came to my productivity.

What I have found interestingly enough is that we know the funk that sometimes those rainy days will put us in, but we never prepare for them in advance. We know how the rain impacts our mood, our emotions, the way we think, but we never think about how that should impact us on the days when it's not raining.

Here's what we normally end up doing, just pushing through it. What does pushing through look like? It looks like someone dragging a kid to the dinner table to eat a bunch of vegetables. It's a struggle.

Struggle is a part of success and I'm not saying we should expect a life without it, but does it have to be the central theme of your life? That I'd argue and say no it does not have to be. This gem helps us to know how to prevent those days from being as frequent as they are. It goes back to the phrase "strike while the iron is hot". It's in the moments when the iron is hot that we need to step on the gas even more and put in the extra work. While you are in the state of flow it's the time to go after it even more so. Why? Because the rainy days are coming. Let me say it again: the R-A-I-N-Y D-A-Y-S A-R-E C-O-M-I-N-G!

The Bible reminds us of the fact that there will be trouble, and our reaction is typically, "Hey, what are you doing here?" like it's some surprise guest that just showed up to your house. Our best approach to ensuring we are going to be unstoppable trains of greatness plowing through every sickness, plowing through every unexpected turn of events, is for us to floor the heck out of that gas pedal when the iron is hot.

What does this look like in a practical way? This is the saving of six months' worth of expenses so if you have to step away from your job or some unexpected changes happen then you are good. Only a person who is putting in the extra work, would be able to do this. Whether it's working more hours or being disciplined enough to tell your money where to go in the form of a budget, instead of having no clue what you spend your money on, this is all the extra work for the rainy days. It is those who put in that extra work that can be found dancing in the rain. It's those who put in that extra work that have peace in the middle of storms. The purpose of this gem is all about giving you peace in the middle of the storm. To allow you to not be in a state of worry.

If you do just enough, then you're only one situation away, one moment away, from being in a situation of "it's not enough." And here's the thing, we, at best, can guess what the weather is going to be. There is no way we can guarantee what the weather will be; however, you can bet your money that bad weather is going to come. So when it's sunny outside, put that little extra work in. When it's sunny and you're doing a mile, push and do 1.25 miles so that you have a 1/4 mile done for the rainy day where you absolutely cannot make it outside.

Here's my promise: you won't regret the extra work you do, you won't say that this was for nothing, because you will do what great people do. Great people prepare and prepare again to ENSURE they go. They do so, by what they do and how much of it they do when the situation is ideal and sunny. My challenge with this gem is that you position yourself today to win for tomorrow and let's dance in the rain.

GEM #5

You Cannot Manage Time, But You Can Spend It.

YOU CANNOT MANAGE TIME, but you can spend it. We always hear: I'm not good at time management; I'm not good at time management; I'm not good at time management. Well, I have good news for you, you cannot be good at time management—it is not possible. It is not possible for you to be good at time management because no matter what it is you do, you cannot manage time. When you have a manager on a job, your manager can tell you what time to work, when to take your lunch break, what time you get off, what activities you should be doing, etc. Isn't that what a manager is doing, checking to make sure that you do things? Well, can I really stop time? No. No matter what I'm going through, I cannot go and say, "Hey, time, listen, I'm going through a lot right now, give me a timeout." The game of life is not like playing a sport, where you can go and call timeout and the referee blows the whistle and says, "Okay, everybody, go to your corners and we will resume in thirty seconds."

The game of life is a non-stop. It will not stop because it's convenient for us. It doesn't work that way. The better way to think about time is thinking about it with the phrase "Time is Money." There is financial management but a more accurate way to view money is the fact we spend it. In the same light, we can look at a day as if it's money. In a day, there are 86,400 seconds, and we can choose how we want to spend them. The interesting thing about time, though, is we do not get to save it. Every day, you get a new 86,400, but yesterday's time is gone, never to be seen again. So the question to ask is: how am I going to spend my time?

When we talk money, we talk about return on investment or (ROI). Where can you spend your time the most to give you more or maximize what it is you're getting?

Are you spending your time on liabilities or assets? Are you spending your time on things that build you up or things that cause you to wither away? Here's a perfect example to help you distinguish between the two. If I spend my time binge watching Netflix, does it produce something? The answer is no. When I'm done watching those shows, that's it. But if I spend my time going ahead, and let's say, create an online course teaching people how to write books, for example—if I spend my time doing that, will that produce something for me in the future? Yeah, it gives me an asset that I can use and leverage to make money while I'm sleeping. Now, I'm spending my time wisely with wisdom, because that time I'm spending to create the course will ultimately buy me back more time in the future where I don't have to work.

What is something you have been spending your time on that you could repurpose? What is something you know that could be of value to someone else if you just packaged them together? Do you know how to kill job interviews? Got a series of tips? You could spend your time creating a guide with those tips and have that sell online 24/7. Maybe it's negotiation tips for black women? One of my best friends Tina had an entire thread going on Facebook that was uplifting and encouraging black women not to settle when it comes to getting a favorable salary. She could turn that into a book, a guide, a workshop, and get a great return on her investment of time. Remember, we can't manage the time, but we sure can spend it in a way that buys us the opportunity to spend our future time differently.

GEM #6

Sometimes The Person That Needs Forgiveness Is You

TELL ME IF YOU'VE heard this statement before, "Forgiveness is not for the other person, forgiveness is for you"? The understanding behind this statement is that if you do not forgive, then you will not be able to move on and will be stuck. As I began to think about this statement, I started to realize there is an assumption made here that if overlooked can be very dangerous. The assumption is that the only person that has ever offended us is someone else. Did you know that **YOU** can offend you?

Are you aware that there are times you can be unloving and unkind to you? Humor me for a moment and consider your past version of you and the current version of you to be two different people. It's easier to think about it this way, and please do not make a face thinking I'm nuts. I promise you this is going somewhere that can help free you and help you get over something that has been holding you back.

Has the past version of you made a decision that today thinking back on it you regret? Like right now as you think about that decision or lack of a decision does it STILL eat at you? If something comes up, there is a chance you have not forgiven yourself for that decision. I can think of many times in my past that I've made a decision that today I call myself stupid for. I think it's important for me to mention this here as a sidebar, you do know that sometimes the decision, the wrong one you made in the past was the best decision you could have made with the wisdom you had at the time? It's like you're calling yourself stupid or saying you should have known better, but that's not fair to your present self, because you did not know!

Too many times we beat ourselves up for what happened, not realizing that the wisdom we now have, that was gifted to you in that experience that you hate.

Many of us just don't receive that because we are too

stuck punishing ourselves instead of forgiving ourselves and giving ourselves grace for the path we took that we had no idea about.

Do you sometimes suffer from taking action, the intentional action we talked about earlier? I bet you it might be because you still have not forgiven yourself for actions you've taken in the past that did not turn out the way you wished. I can see your face right now, you just put the book down, didn't you? This is a praise break moment, a moment to run around the room, throw the book down on the floor if you have to. This gem was designed to free you from the condemnation of your past decisions. I intentionally did not choose the word "mistakes" because I believe that all the decisions we make were for reasons that we may never fully understand, but it gives us something we can use and learn from in the future. It's why I love the phrase, "You win or learn, never lose." Without forgiveness for our past, we lose and never learn how to win. Today, say sorry to you. Say it out loud right now: "(Insert Your Name Here), I'm sorry". If you are really bold and really want to be free, go before a mirror and say, "(Your Name), I forgive you for what happened; you were only doing what you knew. You made the best decision you could with what you had."

If you did that exercise, you are a step closer to creating your masterpiece, because now what was holding you back, is no longer in front of you, now it's behind you. I'm proud you did that courageous act to forgive yourself. Your future self-thanks you.

GEM #7

A Short Word Of Encouragement Goes A Long Way

A SHORT WORD OF encouragement goes a long way. Sometimes, we just don't realize the power of less. We often think that a book of many words is what we need to be encouraged or to have our lives shifted in a positive direction, but that is not necessarily the case. Sometimes just three to four words can change our lives. I think back to how just four words shifted the trajectory of my life when I asked Marsha to marry me. What's crazy is while the question created the opportunity for my life to change, it was her one word response that set it off when she said, "YES!"

Here are some powerful short words of encouragement

that can go a long way:

I love you (3)

Just do it (3)

Yes, I can (3)

Yes (1)

I will (2)

I believe in you (4)

You can do it (4)

Just believe (2)

Yes, you can (3)

I got this (3)

Too many times we think that saying a lot means it's going to do a lot, but that is not necessarily the case. I don't know if you've ever been in a room where you've seen somebody talk too much, and you're like, man, they just think that the longer they talk something is going to hit. That person does not realize that saying more is not helping you be more effective, it's doing the complete opposite. Impact is not just a quantity game, as much as it's a quality game. Sometimes, it can be as short as three words, two words, or even one word.

Maybe today, as you are reading this, you are in need of

an encouraging word. Perhaps you've found yourself in what feels like an impossible situation. Let's pause and park for a moment at that word, impossible. A word that is negative in nature or filled with hopelessness can easily be converted into a word that is positive. Give this a try: If you add an apostrophe between the I and M in the word impossible, you will notice that it says what?

I'MPOSSIBLE.

You see it? The word itself tells you that you are possible. If you feel like you're in an impossible situation, put the apostrophe between the I and the M and remember that it spells I'm possible. No matter what is outside of you telling you that you cannot get it, let me remind you that everything within you can conquer whatever is outside of you. And again, you don't need a lot. You just need the right stuff—the right thing. And so when it comes to encouragement, don't worry about having to say a lot. Sometimes it's just saying hi. Sometimes people just want to be seen. They want to feel like they matter, like you saw them. And so just saying, hello, how are you? How are you really doing? Sometimes it's those three to five words that make somebody feel like, wow, you saw me. Wow, that really touched me.

You look nice.

You have a nice smile.

These are not long words, but I'm telling you if we went on a challenge to go and just say a word to some-body, a word of encouragement, you don't know what that might mean for someone. Let me leave you with this funny quick story that just happened to me recent-ly. There is a lady who lives on my floor, every time she sees me, she always says the same few words. Every time she says it, I get hyped; I get a pep in my step. What does she say? "Look at Mr. Skinny." I have not shared this publicly, but all my life weight loss has been a challenge for me. It's not easy to go to the gym, it's not easy to make the right food choices day in and day out but, boy when that lady says, "Look at Mr. Skinny," that show of encouragement sure goes a long way for me. I've caught myself on days where, with conviction, I said, "I'm not going to the gym," and there she goes on the way to the elevator saying an encouraging word.

It's my hope that you will be encouraged by "I'M POSSIBLE" but that you too will go ahead and en-courage others as well. Let's be the gift that continues to give. The holidays are not the only time we can be merry—that is a cheer we can spread at any time. And the cool part? It doesn't have to be long!

GEM #8

Your Later Is At The Mercy Of Your Now

DO YOU LIKE CANDY?

Growing up, one of my absolute favorite candies were called "Now and Later." If you would have told me that I would reference this candy in a book a few decades later, I would have bet my entire piggy bank on it and would have lost it all.

Here's what I know about your later, it's created in your now. What you future holds is connected to what you put into your present, but not too many people make this connection. Honesty moment here. Have you ever caught yourself anxious about tomorrow? I know I have. I would always think about what I have to do tomorrow, what will three to five years look like, do I have a ten year goal? What about my kids? The list goes on and on. The more I think about the future, the more my anxiety builds.

The solution? The remedy? Focus on right now. It's the only way you can actually impact your future anyway, so why not put all your focus and energy into that? Your future needs you to adapt this mindset. Your future is at the mercy of the moment you're living in right now. If nothing changes right now in this moment, guess what, nothing changes later. I know that is not proper English but I just need to drill home the idea that your later is at the mercy of your now.

It's no surprise to me, that a book called *The Power of Now*, written by Eckhart Tolle, would be a NY Times Best Selling Book, because the power is really in the right now. This book has sold over 2 million copies! I'd love for that kind of reach and impact, wouldn't you? The subtitle of the book is "A Guide To Spiritual Enlightenment." If you want to learn more about this, read the book, but this gem gives you a cliff note that you can wrap your head around: "Your later is at the mercy of your now".

Here are a few questions to ask yourself in regard to this gem. "What do I want to see tomorrow?" After you ponder that question, immediately say to yourself, that answer is at the mercy of this next question: "What am I doing now to get it?" Remember these two questions will always be connected. They are two sides of a same coin, Siamese twins, if you will. Or for a corny television reverse, "You can't have one without the other."

SN: Guess what television show that's from? DM @ geoderice and let me know the answer!

GEM #9

Know What You Don't Want

Do you know what is one of the hardest questions to answer? It's not that complicated math problem where there were numbers and letters in them, it's actually a question that is just four words long: "What Do You Want?" One of my mentors Ryan Lee in a recent email talked about how important this question really is and how it can honestly help provide us with direction to know what we should be doing right now. So I propose to you this question, "What do you want?" If you're like me, this question, while simple, is complex and one that gets me stuck a lot of times. I began to think after some time that it was me, but then I would go to a speaking engagement and ask the audience the very same question, and they, too, were having a hard time answering it. I can remember a talk I gave less than seven days ago, where I asked a student those four words, his reply, "I don't know." Immediately, I saw confusion on his face, almost like he was supposed to have the answer to the question but did not.

So what does someone do in this situation? Do they take that square peg of a question and try to shove it into a triangular empty space? No. Here's a cool hack you can use to help you get from that state of cloudiness to a state of clarity. Ask yourself the opposite. Are you still stuck when asking the question, what you don't want? I am not sure how this idea came to me, but the floodgates opened up for me when I started asking that question. No longer was I stumped. I was easily able to identify the things I don't want. It's like going to a restaurant with my wife or picking a restaurant with her. I'd say, "Hey, babe, where you want to go eat?" and she would reply, "I don't know," but then I would say, "Where do you not want to go?" She would say, "No pizza, no barbecue, no diner, etc." You see with that, I do have something that I can work with and I believe you knowing what you don't want can help you have something to work with, too.

Ask yourself right now, make a list of what you don't want? Is it a work environment that kills your joy?

How about I don't want to live in constant fear of what tomorrow holds? Or I don't want to have jealousy and envy be the fuel that my car runs on?

Once you identified what you don't want, you can simply flip it and discover what it is you do want. This simple gem, helps to unclog your brain and to reverse out of that mental dead end, so you can begin driving toward your destiny again.

GEM #10

You're Guaranteed A Degree When You're Done With School, But Not An Education

RAISE YOUR HAND IF you know someone who went to school, but you wouldn't know it by the way they're living (raises hand).

Isn't it crazy how two people can go to the same school, graduate with the same degree, but one is well-off and the other is not? Now, I know there are circumstances that can come up which can impact the outcome, but the root of this gem comes from the fact that an education and a degree are not the same thing.

There are many educated people who don't have degrees, and many people with degrees that are uneducated. How can this be? What is the difference and how can we apply this to our lives?

I wish I was making this stuff up and that this was not my life story, but this really is. I attended St. John's University, and so did the two friends that I made while there, but I noticed how different our lives were immediately after we graduated. They were a lot further than I was, but we finished the race of getting our degrees at the same time. Years later, I learned that there was something I lacked or did not get and that's an education. I did not get what is called the "hidden curriculum." I only learned what were on the lines, while my two friends learned what were in between the lines and in the margins, too!

We were in the same place, but we did not have the same approach. Their level of engagement was different than mine. I just went and did the assignments as I was told and then left the campus immediately after. Now when I tell this story everyone asks, "Were you a commuter student?" The answer is yes, but SO WERE THEY! Instead of just doing the assignments, they joined clubs, they attended events, asked questions, attended study hall at the library, they were engaged, while at best, I was flirting if you even want to call it that.

They were curious and wanting all they could get out of their experience, while I was just focused on the degree itself. Since then, I've shared this with anyone who wants to listen: Being curious is an amazing trait to have. Ask questions, play the "but why" game you used to do as kids. Question everything if you have to, but don't settle for the off the rack experience, that's the cheap one.

For you, I want you to have a rich experience. I want nothing left behind, nothing overlooked. Engage in what you are doing, do not settle for just knowing about it, understand it.

Be curious! Curiosity kills the cat, but it makes a lot of millionaires. A lot of people who created million dollar businesses have achieved amazing success because they were curious—they didn't miss the hidden curriculum, the hidden agendas, the things that no one is talking about. They made sure that those were conversations they were present in.

I want to make sure you really get this, so let me drive this point home with this illustration. Remember when you used to do math in school? Do you remember how we had to show our work? Knowing the answer was not enough, we had to show how we arrived at that answer? I used to think these teachers were so annoying. I got the answer, isn't that what matters? What I did not know was the hidden curriculum, the hidden agenda, the hidden gem they were trying to teach me. I thank my math teachers now for letting me know if I understand the process, I can always get the answer and when I don't get the right answer, the process itself will reveal to me why. But if you just blindly copy the answer on the paper next to you, you'll always be lost. Seek understanding like it's a million dollars, because that will pay huge dividends for you in the future. HUGE!!!

GEM #11

The Practice Is Always Longer Than The Game.

3 YEARS???

That was my reaction when I took a masterclass by movie producers Spike Lee and Judd Apatow. What made me react this way was hearing how long it took for a movie to go from idea to the screen for both you and I to watch it. Can you imagine that in two hours I can watch three years' worth of work? This is the trick of success. It's here and gone in a flash but what we don't realize is how long it took to get to there.

Take for example, the Super Bowl, which unfortunately, my team the Indianapolis Colts didn't make. It takes practically an entire year filled with weight-lifting sessions, film sessions, training camp, pre-season and sixteen grueling weeks of a season, plus playoffs to get there, but to us it's a three hour show. I share this gem because I want you to not fall into the trap of thinking about the game so much that you do not acknowledge the practice that it takes to get there. I also share this gem for you to get perspective about the process. When you start to think what is taking so long, I want you to remember that the practice is supposed to be longer than the game. When you feel like time has stood still and it even feels like you have been forgotten or trampled over, I want you to know that the practice is always longer than the game.

Malcolm Gladwell in his book *Outliers* talks about how it takes 10,000 hours to become an expert, and sometimes when hearing that I honestly get discouraged. Who has 10,000 hours? I have like one hour, can I get a witness?! That's literally about eleven years if you spent every single waking moment on it. But I then remember the quote by the great Muhammad Ali, "I hated every minute of training, but I said, don't quit, suffer now and live the rest of your life as a champion." So I share that with you now. Do not be discouraged that the practice is longer, because when the game comes you will get your moment. Do not overlook the process and what it's helping you to become. Heck, I'm happy the practice is this long when it comes to our doctors, aren't you? Could you imagine if your doctor was able to get certified in just a few hours? That doctor isn't operating on me!

Likewise, take this pearl of wisdom, take the virtue of patience and pack it in your bag, so that when the moment comes for the game, you'll be refined, sharpened and ready to go. That is my hope for you.

Pick up that thing you quit on, pick it up right now. I know you spent a while at it, but go a little while longer, keep putting in your hours, the expert title, the Super Bowl, your movie, it's coming; in fact, it's waiting on you.

They say greatness takes time and it's not available at a discount. You're a luxury that's worth the wait.

GEM #12
Done Is The New Perfect

I KNOW YOU'VE HEARD it. Perfection doesn't exist but it doesn't stop us from pursuing it, right? No matter how many times we look at something, we can always find something that could be tweaked, can't we? That is the perfectionist in both you and I that just won't let us be. Why are we like this? This is the question I had when I put my curiosity hat on. I could not accept this to be something I know and do nothing about. As I began to ask questions, answers started to appear.

You want to know one of the reasons why you and I seek perfection all the time, even to a fault? Because we know that if it's 100 percent pure, then no one can judge us on it. Did I hit a nerve there, or what? You cannot see me, but I had to take a break from typing and let that sit in my spirit. The fear of being judged is at the root of my desire to be perfect. We use perfection as an insurance policy so that we won't get hurt or criticized for what we've done.

Have you ever seen someone who has all the potential in the world, but just won't ever press the send button? It's because of this. Their need for protection through perfection stops them. The thinking, although they don't realize it, is if I don't put it out there, you cannot judge me on whether it's good, bad, or perfect. Does this resonate with you? Maybe it's a sixty second video you need to record and post on social media that takes you 100 takes to do, or it's a great movie script on your computer that is still in draft mood, or that request you want to ask which you have not pushed send on yet.

Want to hear the kicker about being in this position? That "protection" you have, isn't protection at all. People will judge you anyway for not pressing send. You'll be judged for pressing send and you'll be judged for not pressing send, so what should you do? Let go of the need to be perfect. Let go of the need to always be right. Stop letting perfection prevent you from seeing your promise.

God uses imperfect people all the time to do His perfect will, so why should you, human, try to be perfect FIRST then go and do whatever it is you were meant to do. Instead, I encourage you to adopt the mentality of PERFECTING. Perfecting is you working toward perfection without the requirement of it to move forward. Perfecting is all about learning as you go. It's applying what Carol Deck in her book *Mindset* calls the "growth mindset." Your best work is ahead of you, so the only way to ever see it is to keep on going. Could you imagine if I waited for perfection to put together this book? (In Hindsight, I kind of did.) You would be missing out from applying these in your life and then others would have missed seeing you apply them and then they would not have a model to follow and the cycle of "protection by perfection" becomes the barrier that keeps us from being our best.

Be okay with progression. As one of my mentors Paul would say, "Geo, it's progression over perfection." I am not into tattoos, but if I were, that would be one I would highly consider getting on my arm, because it's something we cannot be reminded of enough.

Get it done. That's the new perfect.

GEM #13

Even Waste Has Purpose, So Best Believe You Do, Too!

CAN I KEEP IT real with you? Despite the motivational videos, quotes, and sayings there are moments of my life where I feel worthless. There are moments in my life where I feel insignificant, lonely, less than, not worthy, the list goes on and on. These feelings suck, there is no two ways to feel about it. It is in those moments this gem has been my saving grace. This gem is where I am reminded of how waste doesn't expire as waste, that it is turned into something else.

The waste of cows, for example, is used as fertilizer! Not a pretty picture, I know, but it's crazy how the waste of a cow can be turned into a nutrient-rich fertilizer that is EXCELLENT for the growth of green plants. Please read those words again. I'm waiting, did you read them? I want you to realize that if cow waste can be not just good, but EXCELLENT for GROWTH of green plants, then you, my friend, are not waste. I don't care what words you may have heard in the school playground that no one cares about you, that you are not worth anything or the words maybe a parent said in the heat of an argument. You have purpose. You are a creation by God and not by accident either. You might feel that you are a mistake, but please let me encourage you to know that in God's hands mistakes are turned into masterpieces all the time. In fact, in the Bible, Ephesians 2 verse 10, it says, "For we are God's masterpiece. He has created us anew in Christ Jesus so we can do the good things he planned for us long ago." I love this verse, not only because I'm God's masterpiece and so are you, but also because it goes to show that you and I are not a mistake. When were the plans made? LONG AGO! This means that you being on this earth is an intentional action that took place. You, my friend, are no accident, no mistake, and you were made to fulfill a purpose. The only job you have to do is be open to receiving what that purpose is. Now, I will warn you that sometimes when we seek purpose in one direction and it does not pan out, we can think that we don't have any purpose or we are not worth much. That could not be further away from the truth. Sometimes those closed doors are really the things we need to find what we are meant to do. This reminds me of a video that the Rock, Dwayne Johnson, put up, which I literally watched last night (crazy how all this connects). In the video, he talked about how he was in Vancouver, one of his favorite places. He shared how he was a professional football player for the Canadian Football League and how he knew he was destined to make it to the NFL. Long story short, he ended up getting cut twice while out there and was left with seven dollars in his pocket. At that moment, you could imagine he probably felt like a waste, but look at him now. He attributes those closed doors to him finding the room that he belonged in, wrestling and acting and building companies left and right, making history all over the place. Heck, people even want him to run for President, not something you hear people say about football players! I say this to let you know that you have purpose and shouldn't be discouraged or ever question if you do. Remember the cow waste, it helps green plants GROW, you too have something special that's worth being called a masterpiece of God.

GEM #14

Preparation Is Just A Public Display To The Thing You Want That You're Getting Ready

WHAT DOES A BABY shower mean? If you said that a baby is coming, you got the right answer. A baby shower is a public display that a couple makes for what is coming—the baby. Preparation is not a sexy term; it's not something we love, and it goes with the gem about the practice is longer than the game. It takes time, but here is the thing I learned from a football player about preparation. The football player was Baltimore Ravens Linebacker Ray Lewis. He shared that he lives by the Five Ps.

Proper

Preparation

Prevents

Poor

Performance

I would later learn this is something that members of the military live by as well. I'm not sure who came up with it first, but the principle means that if we want to perform well, then we must properly prepare. Have you ever had a moment where you felt like your ass was out? A situation where you were not prepared or caught off guard? I have and it was one of the most embarrassing moments in my speaking career. I was not as prepared as I should have been and boy did it show. Where was this gem back then? I remember feeling shame, but the reality was I shouldn't have been surprised. I was not getting ready. What receipts of preparation did I have?

When it comes to preparation, it's hard for us to relate to it because it's a thing and not human. You can understand hurting someone feelings, but you won't understand if I told you I let opportunity down. It's in these moments that I apply personification.

Personification, as you may already know, is giving human-like characteristics and traits to something that is non-human. In fact, I did this with one of my clients. She was having a hard time going to the gym, so we applied personification and gave her gym a name. I knew that she did not like letting PEOPLE down but would give herself a pass if the only person she was letting down was herself.

The purpose of this gem is for you to be convicted, found guilty of the very thing you say you want to pursue. This is a concept I refer to in my first book, *The Thirst Is Real*. If I pop a reality tape of your life in, will I find evidence that the thing you're longing for you're putting in the preparation to acquire it?

For example, when I said I wanted to run my first 5k, if you popped in the video of my life, you would see me texting my friend Glenn who is a runner and asking him about what races are available, you can see him giving me suggestions of what running sneakers to get and where to get them from. All of these things were preparation. It was me publicly displaying to the 5k or Mister 5k that I'm getting ready. I then went ahead and began running on the treadmill, more evidence that I was getting ready. If you do not have what you want, go back to the video tape and replay it, that is probably why the later you that you have been longing for is still not a part of the present you. Do not sleep on preparation, doing so will only leave you living out anything BUT a dream when you're awake. Put in the work, have your shower for what you are looking forward to, and let the world know you're getting ready.

GEM #15

It's Always Hard To Find Something You Were Never Looking For

DO YOU REMEMBER THE game Punch Buggy? My shoulders cannot forget it! Just in case you do not know the game, it's a car game that I played while I was a child where we would punch a person whenever we spotted a Volkswagen Beetle. Back then, and still to a point now, you did not see these cars often, so the thought is that you won't ever get punched. You were only punched if the other person spotted one. I remember thinking how I would never get punched because these cars were rare, and I never saw them. An interesting thing happened, though, whenever we played the game, someone would always spot a Beetle—every freaking time someone would spot one! It's as if the driver of the Beetle was told exactly what our bus route would be, because EVERY TIME one would be spotted. Over time we decided we were spotting too many of them, so we decided to go ahead and add colors to it. Now, for sure, we should not find a red Beetle or a blue Beetle or a green Beetle, right? WRONG!!! Still my arm was getting punches. How in the world could this be happening? This is where our gem comes into play. "It's always hard to find something you were never looking for." Because we were looking for the Beetles, we found them. Could it really be that simple? Yes, it can be. By introducing the thought of the Beetle, we set our brain in motion to find them and find them the brain did. Thinking back on it, this feels like a magic trick, but it's crazy how powerful this computer in our heads really is.

If just searching helps us to find, then what do we need to do? Introduce what you are looking for. If you look for the right things you will find it. I think of questions we sometimes ask ourselves such as, "Why am I poor?" Isn't it crazy how our brain always has an answer for that? What I've realized about the brain is that it's super obedient. It does not overwrite your question, it simply answers it. The same brain when asked, "how come I'm so wealthy", will also go ahead in search of the answer. Give it a try, this stuff is amazing when you put it into practice. Anything that has been out of your grasp, there is a good chance you're simply not looking for it, or you have not been searching for it long enough. It's there, whatever you want is there, just like those yellow Volkswagen Beetles were! I still can't believe that happened, but you can help to stir your mind in the right direction by telling it what to look for.

Don't expect it to do it on its own, though, and don't fall victim of what you told it before. Ask regularly, give it the destination you desire today and see how you begin to get the directions to getting there.

GEM #16

We Are Products Of Our Past, But We Don't Have To Be Prisoners Of It

TELL ME IF YOU'VE heard the following quotes:

"Only a fool trips over what is behind him."

"If the past calls you, send it to voicemail because it has nothing new to tell you."

"The rearview mirror is smaller than the windshield window because you're going forward not backwards."

All of these are quotes that speak to the past, and these are all quotes that I've said with my coaching clients or in a speech. If you were one of them, allow me to apologize here if I made you feel like your past never happened. These quotes can easily make someone think that their past should have no impact on them at all, and that is not true. Our past is not some made up event that we can delete; it happened to us and has helped shape who we are today, both good and bad. Sometimes we disregard our past to our detriment because we are bombarded with messages and messengers who tell us to forget about the past like it does not exist. I've realized after working with people who have had some challenging pasts that is not easy to do, nor is it beneficial to just disregard what happened to them. Where the shift comes and where I do stand today is that we are products of our pasts, but we do not have to be prisoners of the past.

Let's say for example you were raised without a father in your life, studies would say that you're less likely to succeed or you will have more problems in life. While this can be true, it does not have to be. That is what you are a product of, but it doesn't have to be where you live. We cannot edit the past, but we can create the future.

I know in your past there were times you threw your whole self at something only to fall straight on your face. What are you supposed to do now? Stay down? You could, but then you might miss out on all the good things that are around you if you only got up. Getting knocked down in your past does not make you a failure. Let me say that again, the failed relationship, the failed marriage, does not have to the period of your life. It does not have to be the end. You can change gears as we talked about in an earlier gem. You can free yourself from the bondage of what was, and grab hold to what could be. It might require forgiveness of others, it might require forgiveness of yourself, but we should not allow anything to keep us in captivity. Your future has something new for you, don't let yesterday take up all the space in your head. The past is real, don't delete it, but don't also delete your future because of it. You are meant for more.

GEM #17

Even A Broken Clock Is Right Twice A Day

THIS GEM IS ABSOLUTELY one of my favorites. My goodness is this a gem, if I've ever seen one. This one is especially for those like me who feel that everything has to be right before moving forward. These are for the people who won't move until all the ducks are in a row. Before I go further please don't think that I subscribe to the school of if it's broken just leave it there and don't fix it, but as I discussed earlier, perfection is not protection. It can lead to prevention of you realizing a better version of you.

This gem is just a reminder that even if we not perfect, we can still be right. Even if you are not perfect, you can still be trending in the right direction. The broken clock being right twice a day, just reminds us that all is not lost if we are not 100 percent fixed. Even if you're not the most effective version of yourself yet, you may not be the most efficient, but you can still get things done. Again, I don't want you to go and fall into the trap of being a functional person, you know, those who are functional alcoholics, or those who can still function despite the addictions that they may have. By no means do I want the addiction to take you over. I want you to always be in control. But at the same time, I don't want you to be so controlling to the point where you need perfection in order to move you. I want you to move in spite of the fact that you're not perfect, yet.

Listen, a baseball player, when he's hitting the ball three out of ten times is a potential Hall of Famer. No basketball players ever shot 100 percent of their shots and made them. Kobe Bryant ranks near the top of the list for most shots missed and still people would sign him up any day of the week to join his team. Let this encourage you to not need it to be 100 percent to make it work. This is not like downloading a file on your computer where if it's at 99 percent, because you won't be able to use it. Continue to get better, continue to improve, fix it little by little, but still be doing something so that you are constantly making progress. Remember: progression over perfection. And then as you continue to get better, you will make greater strides; you'll improve things better over time, but don't stop. Don't do nothing. Do something because your future self is really depending on you to do so. So, again, remember: even a broken clock is right twice a day, so you don't have to be completely fixed to get it right.

GEM #18

The Answer You Are Looking For Is Waiting For Your Question. Don't Ask, Don't Get.

ACE HOOD, I OWE you some credit for this one, man. It was Ace Hood the rapper who uttered this infamous line:

"Closed mouths don't get fed on this boulevard."

This line meant that if you did not open your mouth, you did not eat. Another quote I read from Mark Batterson, who wrote the book *Draw The Circle*, said, "The greatest tragedy in life is the prayers that go unanswered because they go unasked." Can you imagine that the life you are living or lack thereof is a result of our reluctance to ask? That would crush me for someone to need something from me, something that I have and the only reason they did not get it was because they did not ask.

Perhaps you've faced this crushing blow, too, because you stopped asking. Perhaps you lost faith in asking the question because you have yet to see the answer. I get it, waiting can be painful. Or not seeing the answer we wanted soon enough stops us from asking the questions we need to, but we must keep the faith. We must keep believing that the answer will come, and it will—if we keep the question coming. They call it Q & A for a reason. Ask the question and you will get the answer.

Personal development guru Tony Robbins who has helped many people live quality lives, once said, "Quality questions create quality lives." In addition, he mentioned that successful people ask better questions and, thus, get better answers. Do you know how to get better at asking questions? By asking. There is no secret recipe for it, ask enough times and you will get feedback on what works and what does not. Ask better questions and you will get better answers but you need to ask questions period. Do not shut yourself off from a better life—a life that will make the years of the past jealous all because you were too hurt or prideful to ask.

If you don't know something, ask. If you have something you need ask, ask, ask, ask. If knowledge is power, then "ask" stands for always seeking knowledge. Do not compromise your power by keeping your mouth closed, because as Ace Hood said, you won't get fed. Your lack of asking just might be the reason why your life looks malnourished.

If someone has let you down from asking, or made you feel dumb for not knowing, that doesn't mean you should stop asking, it just means you asked the wrong person. All it takes is one YES to change your life and erase all the NOs.

Let's EAT!

GEM #19

If you wait until you feel like it, you'll never have it.

LATELY, I'VE BEEN ON a health kick as you may know, and it's been amazing to see the transformation. It was not easy, but it's been so rewarding. There is a part of this health kick, though, that people may not be aware of.

I believe many think that when I wake up, when my alarm goes off, that I am super excited, and I feel like getting out of my warm bed next to Marsha (my wife) and jump into my clothes, get in the car smiling ear to ear excited to go to the gym. This IS NOT how I go to the gym in the morning. In fact, one of my best friends and I talk about how we feel before going to the gym all the time and it looks NOTHING like how we look when we are done.

Here's what it looks like:

{Alarm goes off}

{Hit snooze button}

{Hit snooze button again}

{Hit snooze button again}

{Get the look of death from our wives if we let that alarm go off one more time}

{Looks for workout clothes}

{Can't find workout clothes so decide were not meant to be to go to the gym that day}

{Then realize that your health is a requirement, not an option, so you search a little longer and find the clothes}

{You struggle into the gym}

~ Sixty minutes later ~

{Super hyped, telling everyone on IG to go to the gym, step on the scale smiling, and saying to yourself I cannot wait to go back tomorrow}

~Repeat~

I apologize for using paper to map this out but it's so important that you realize, if I waited for the feelings to go to the gym to come, I would have never gone. Even forty pounds lighter, I still have episodes that look like above, but the feeling afterward is what I chase.

Feelings later, commitments now. This is how you want to approach things. If not, then you might just be waiting for a long period of time and I'm not sure how much time you have. I even once coined the phrase #NoDrake in one of my speeches because of this whole idea that I need to feel it then I will act. Drake has the song "In My Feelings," and I wanted to help those who follow me know that if you wait on your feelings, you may never be able to live in your dreams. You'll just watch them from the window.

I want you to not have dreams; I want you living in them. This is the time to start living that out.

GEM #20

Can't find what you love? Find what you hate and do the opposite.

IF YOU CANNOT FIND what you love, find what you hate, and do the opposite. This kind of ties back to an earlier gem. In play here are two emotions—love and hate. Emotions are energies, but rarely do we acknowledge the energy that hate can provide us. While hate has a negative connotation, many movements that have been positive have been a result of hate. Sometimes we are stuck in not knowing what we love, or we have trouble expressing that love or we lack clarity in identifying what we love. In those cases, we can simply borrow the energy that hate creates by identifying what we hate, or as we said in an earlier gem, what you don't want. Once you find what you don't want then just to do the opposite.

Here's an example. I hate feeling broke. If you hate feeling broke, what do you love (the opposite)? The opposite of being broke or feeling broke is being or feeling wealthy. If I dig deeper, what I really love is financial freedom, but without looking at what I hate first, I was not able to get there. If what you love comes easily, please go there, but if you are stuck not knowing what you love, then use this tactic as a way to help free your mind and begin thinking of things. Jot them down, if you need to, and then ask yourself what the opposite of that is. Consider this gem a strategy to warming up your love car so that it's not cold and won't break down.

What do you hate? Make a list on a separate sheet of paper and then draw another column where you ask yourself what the opposite of that is. This will help you to build your love list, so you can know exactly what the things you love are and solely chase after those.

GEM #21

The path of least resistance isn't always the best path.

THEY SAY FOOTBALL IS a lot like life and boy did it teach me this gem—the path of least resistance isn't always the best path. There I was, on a football field playing defensive tackle—that's the guy who is right in front of the ball on the defensive side. My job is to hit the guy with the ball, be it the quarterback, running back, tight end, or wide receiver. On this particular play, the ball was given to the running back and the blocker in front of me let me go without laying a hand on me (a.k.a. no resistance). My eyes lit up as I saw myself making a huge play to stop the ball carrier, but that moment never came. Why? It was a big ol' trap. The path of least resistance was a setup as the pulling guard from the opposite side came and hit me on my blind side, knocking me off my feet. That day, I learned that just because it looks easy, does not mean it's the best.

Many times if something is hard, we immediately think that it is not for us. But, what if the opposite is actually true? You might be reading this right now saying to yourself, "Geo, the challenges I'm facing … it's just too much. Maybe this is not what I was meant to do." To that, I would say, if the road being challenging is the only reason, then maybe you are EXACTLY where you need to be. Challenging tough roads, make tough people. There's a saying: "A smooth sea never made a skillful sailor." What if the challenging road was there to help you get to the best version of you?

I believe this is one of the biggest traps we face and prevents us from being able to find the best us. When the road is easy, there is no rising to the occasion—there is no skill needed. I don't know why we are wired this way, but we seem to transform, we get our testimonies only after we've been tested. Don't always go for the easy road. Les Brown says, "If you do what is easy, life will be hard, if you do what is hard, life will be easy". I'm not glorifying struggle, but I am asking if you would be willing to go there if it will unlock the best version of you. Nothing should stop you from growing, not even a path of resistance. Level up, allow your faith and your spirit to be strengthened by what you go through and don't take the path that will shrink or stunt your growth.

GEM #22

You can't catch the new while holding onto the old.

I FIRST HEARD THIS while I was watching a sermon by Pastor Bishop TD Jakes. In the sermon, he has an illustration where he had a beach ball in his hand, and he had another person he was talking to who also had a beach ball in their hand. He then explained how the person who had the beach ball in their hand, let's call it his old, while TD Jakes' beach ball was his new. He then threw the ball to the guy who had to drop his ball so he could catch the ball TD Jakes threw. That is when he explained that it would not have been possible for the guy to catch the new if he was still holding onto the old. This illustration really drove home the idea that until we let go of the old stuff, there will be no room for the new stuff.

Sometimes what that looks like is forgiving yourself like we talked about in a previous gem. Sometimes that's not being so fixed on what it looks like, but being more led by the vision of what could be. My pastor shared with me a great book called *Visioneering* by Andy Stanley and it talks about vision and focusing ourselves on what should be and what could be. Without us letting go of the old, what should be and could be will never be. This is why this book was so great. I would hate for you to miss a new thing because you we're stuck on the old thing. From glory to glory we go, the Bible says, so why not let that be what you experience in your life, too.

Here is my question for you—what new thing do you want to catch? And what old thing are you willing to let go to ensure that you're able to catch that new thing? What are you willing to let go? I love the part in the Bible in Isaiah 43:19 where it says, "For I am about to do something new, See I have already begun! Do you not see it?" You won't see it if your eyes are fixed on what was. Let God do something new in your life.

GEM #23

Fix the roof while its sunny

HAVE YOU EVER BEEN in a HAVE TO situation before? Who likes that? If we could, we would all want to be in situation where we did what we wanted because we wanted to and not because we had to. The worst time to fix something is when you NEED it to be fixed.

Take for example getting an oil change. It's said that every 3000 miles you should get your oil change, that is what mechanics suggest, but how many times do we go and wait until the maintenance light comes on to do it? By the time the light comes on, there is a good chance you might have created other issues because you were late to address the issue when you could have.

You want to be proactive. Doing so prevents you from being in a position when you have to do something whether you are willing or not. This is where the idea of fix the roof while it's sunny comes from. To fix the roof when it's raining is no fun. You get all wet, the things in the house get water damage because of the rain, it makes a bad situation even worst.

But, if you fix the roof when it is sunny, you do not need things to go perfectly. It's weird how when we have to fix stuff, everything has to go right just to make sure it all does not go wrong. Who wants that kind of pressure? I can recall many times not fixing issues when I was aware of them and leaving them for later on. Am I the only one?

I was reading a book called *Relentless* not too long ago where the author Tim Grover talked about putting things off for later. To give you context, Tim Grover was the personal trainer of three of the best basketball players of all time, Michael Jordan, Kobe Bryant and Dwayne Wade.

Tim talked about putting things on the back burner, only one thing can happen to that thing—it cools off. That cannot be good and is definitely a lot harder to handle when they cool off. You want to strike the iron while it's hot or do what you have to do when you spot it before it makes a bigger spot. This is the idea behind the gem: "Fix the roof while it's sunny."

What roofs have you been neglecting to fix? You know what I'm talking about. That stuff you said you would get to, that stuff that has remained on your to-do list month after month, year after year. Do not let it get to the point that it is frozen for you to go ahead and act on it. That is like trying to cook dinner, but you just took the chicken out the freezer. It's not a good look. Put the chicken out long before you need to cook it, or you and your company will be starving. I use food for an example here but take this as a kind warning to not starve yourself from the things that matter most to you.

GEM #24

Information without application leads to frustration.

ARE YOU FAMILIAR WITH the term information obesity? Information obesity is someone who consumes a lot of information and never uses it. This is similar to obesity that we know where someone carries too much body fat, which leads to a ton of health issues. Information obesity can do a number on one's mental health. Having some fat is not a bad thing, we all have to have some fat, but too much of it is not good for us, and the same goes for information. Accumulating too much information but never applying it will leave you frustrated.

This creates a dangerous illusion where you feel like

you should have more because you know more, but that is not what it takes to have more. Having more comes directly from the information we apply, not the information we accumulate. I once sat in a room where one of my mentor's asked how many of us know someone who is super smart or who knows a lot, but their life doesn't match what they know. Everybody in the room raised their hand. This is a perfect example of what information alone will do. It's good to know, but it is better to know-know and that only comes from doing what you know.

Knowing is simply not enough. Having access to information is not enough either. If access alone was the key to being successful then the most important place to be in the world would be the library, but that is not the case.

Those who are successful, don't live in libraries. Instead, you can find them out on the field applying what was found in the books. This is what creates the haves versus the have nots. This is one of the keys to avoiding a life of frustration. This is what allows super successful people the opportunity to continue to acquire new information. It's because they used the old information already, so there is room to catch the new information and apply it.

So what am I saying to you right now? Stop accumulating more information, stop trying to get more information, instead start applying what you already know. You already have enough information to get you to where your next stop ought to be. Don't get more information, do more of what you already know. Do not be the kind of person who has ten books they have not read, yet still sign up for a book of the month subscription program. This is only going to make you more frustrated because the action of getting more books will once again create the illusion that you are getting closer to success, but no action has really taken place.

Move away from the shiny object syndrome. This is something I used to get caught up in a lot. Remember torrents? I used to have access to a secret website where I could download a ton of personal development stuff. In fact, I got hundreds of hours of content, but guess which ones changed my life? The ones I applied!

What piece of information that you already know, will you apply next? This is the key to unlocking another level of your potential.

GEM #25

Don't go through problems only, grow through them, too.

TAKE A LOOK AT this conversation.

Person 1: Hey, man, how you doing?

Person 2: I'm all right, man, just going through it.

Do you know someone who all the time when you talk to them they just go through stuff? Can you recall a time you were that person—a person who just seems to have life throw the kitchen sink at them? We've all been there a time or two where it just seems like going through stuff is magnetic to us. If it's not one thing, then it's another. We will all go through problems, few people will grow through them though.

Perhaps for many, they can only see the obstacles and miss the opportunities the obstacles often present. Every obstacle you face comes with its seed of opportunity. At first, I did not understand this, but reading the book *Think and Grow Rich* by Napoleon Hill, he shared this concept about how if we pay attention, we can use the obstacles we face to help us get to the next level. The trick with all of this is being aware that the opportunities for growth, are embedded in the obstacles. They are not obvious, it's not on the label, you have to unwrap the obstacle to find it.

It would be nice if when we faced obstacles that they would declare from the start that it is there to build us up, but it does not work that way. It takes books, like the one you are holding right now, to remind you, and this is how we often grow.

These problems that we face are not here to defeat us. They're there to make us. They're there to refine us, they're there to sharpen us.

The next time a problem comes, I want you to smile. Yes, people will think you're nuts, people will think you are crazy, they won't get you at first, but you have foresight and you know what it is. They see obstacle, but you know there is a seed of greatness, a seed of opportunity embedded on the inside of that obstacle. Don't throw away the obstacle, do not rush to get rid of it, for doing so will be you forfeiting the formula you need to grow and get to the next level.

Your future self needs you to take on this milk so you can become big and strong.

GEM #26

You can have whatever you want if you are willing to pay the price.

ONE SUMMER, THERE WAS a song that no one could tell me to shut off. What song was this? T.I.'s "Whatever You Like." I don't know what it is about the song, maybe because I love shopping sprees or something, but that song did it for me back in those days. Listening to it the other day, though, I had an epiphany.

Unfortunately, the song has left many people forgetting there is a second part to "you can have whatever you like" and that's the fact that someone has to pay for whatever you like. Whatever you like is not something that is free. Even if the person T.I. was rapping about can get whatever they want, T.I. has to swipe that card for them to get it. This is a missing link that many people overlook. You cannot have whatever you like and pay whatever you want to get it. Don't I wish it worked that way! I wish I could pay $10 for something that is worth $100.

Greatness is one of those things that rarely goes on sale or comes at a cheaper price. Take for example the Apple iPhone. That's a great phone (Samsung lovers, leave me alone). When was the last time you saw an iPhone at 50 percent off, or 60 percent off? Next to never. If you want to product, you have to pay the sticker price, period!

Anything worth having comes at a price. If you're willing to pay it, THEN and only THEN can you have whatever you like. The whatever is tied to you keeping that same energy and saying you'll pay whatever it costs to get it.

When Michael Phelps wanted to win those gold medals, that is what he wanted, but at what COST? Training hours upon hours, eating almost 10,000 calories so he does not lose any muscle? He got what he wanted, because he was willing to pay the price it cost to get it. What is it that you want? What does it cost? Are you willing to pay that price for it? If the answer is yes, you're willing, then it's inevitable you will get it.

You want to be your boss? Is that your "whatever you like" and are you willing to pay the price of uncertainty? Are you willing to pay the price of putting yourself out there? No matter what you want, you can have if you are willing to pay the price to get it. There is nothing too expensive to those who are willing to put in the work and pay the price. I do not judge people who have lavish things, they knew what they wanted and were willing to pay the price. More power to them. Some people will look at you dropping $6 for a Mango Dragon fruit at Starbucks to be too much, but, hey, you were willing to pay the price for that, so you can have whatever you like.

Apply this same principle to anything you want in life—it's really a formula that works no matter what. Sub what you want in the blank, and then where it says costs, put "whatever it takes" in that place. When that is your answer, the want will always take care of itself.

GEM #27

You can't unlock the door to your dreams by putting the key only halfway in.

THERE ARE TWO CHOICES in life, what are they?

Option 1: Go All Out

Option 2: To Hold Back

This is something the great sports psychologist professor Dr. Rob Gilbert shared with me when I attended a seminar that he was running. It's simple but yet complex. He shared that no matter what it is we do, it always comes down to one of those two choices. Are you going to hold back (leave something in reserve) or are you going to go all out (leave nothing in reserve)?

Those who go all out, they are the ones who can stand at the end of the journey victorious or defeated and say they have absolutely no regret. Do you want a life of no regrets? Or do you want to bear the weight of them? There's a saying that the weight of discipline weighs ounces, but the weight of our regrets weighs tons. I would hate for you to walk around with something that weighs tons! This is where this gem comes in. How does one ensure they achieve all they can, unlocking their full potential? By putting the key ALL THE WAY IN. A key put halfway, unlocks nothing. Try it the next time you attempt to open a door. Hold back the key versus going all out with it and see if anything unlocks. The answer is: it won't.

What if the thing that's been preventing you from unlocking your dreams is the decision to go all out, to fully engage and leave nothing in reserve—to say that I'm going to give it everything that I have so that I can hold my head up high and say I have zero regrets? How amazing would it feel to be light from the ounces of discipline instead of being weighed down by the tons of regret.

The goal is for you to press on and run toward the prize that is set before you and the best way I know to do that is to fully engage and not go halfway. Even the best of the best cannot succeed by going halfway. I remember reading a story about Oprah and how going halfway almost cost her one of her dreams.

The Discovery Network offered Oprah her own network partnering with her on the network we know today as OWN. Out of the gate the network struggled. A big reason for the struggle was the fact that OWN was in LA, yet Oprah was in Chicago. She was not fully engaged in what was happening because she was in a long distance relationship with her network. Discovery then simply asked Oprah a question, "No hard feelings if you don't want to, but do you want to do this for real, or not? If you do, we are going to need you to be here, remote access won't cut it." They basically told her that we need you to go all-in, and that she did. With her network now profitable and thriving, I firmly believe it's because she decided to stop going halfway. She went all the way in and unlocked the full potential of her network.

I cannot help but think how many people benefited from her making that decision. I cannot help but think how many people could benefit from you making the same decision Oprah made?

It's time you ask yourself the question Dr. Rob says will

determine whether you succeed or not—will you go all out, or will you hold back?

The choice is *yours*.

GEM #28

Successful people have bigger "Don't do lists" than To Do Lists."

WANT TO KNOW THE secret to successful people? It has less to do with what they do and more to do with what they don't do! A perfect example of this is asking a fit guy or girl what it take to be lean. I'm not talking about kind of in shape, I'm talking about the epitome of health and fitness. If *Shape Magazine* or *Men's Fitness* was looking for a cover model, these would be the people they would go after. We know that exercise and eating well are both things that contribute to great health, but what blows me away is how simple the secrets to success really are. Ask any of them what they eat, and you will find that they don't eat much. Here's what a breakdown might sound like:

Breakfast:

Egg whites, oatmeal

Lunch:

Chicken breast, green veggies, and brown rice.

Dinner:

Fish, green veggies

Snacks:

Low fat Greek yogurt or a protein shake that is low in sugar.

They then repeat this over and over and over again day in and day out.

Not a lot, right? Pretty simple, even boring. Ask them what they don't eat, and the list is out of this world—no bread, no simple carbs, no fried foods, no juices, no cookies, no ice cream, no sweets, the list goes on and on. This gave me a glimpse of what successful people have compared to those that are not successful. Successful people have smaller "to do lists" and larger "don't do lists".

Is your to-do list super long? Maybe it's time to cut that list in half and start building your "don't do list" up. Successful people use their yes or to-do list like it's scarce because they know depth and quality trumps surface level and quantity. Reading this, I hope it encourages you to start building what I call "Positive FOMO." That's missing out on the things that don't matter and making sure you fear missing out on the things that do. This is what separates the successful from the ones that aren't.

Every time I speak to my millionaire mentors and ask them about what favorite shows they watch, at best they might have one, while the average person has like 5-6 shows and binge watch a ton of others. Limit the list and you will remove the limits of your success. Applying this gem will increase your productivity, help you become more present to the things that matter most and help transform your life like very few things can.

Do not read any further without starting to write your "don't do list." The success you've been waiting for is counting on you to do so.

GEM #29

Lies Over Time Become True

Are you a liar?

I know that is a weird question to ask and no one would admittingly say they are, but you've told a lie every now and then, haven't you? Be it a white lie or a real lie, we've all said things that are not true, but what happens when we continue to say it over and over again? It goes from a lie to your truth.

I can remember a point in time when I used to speak things over myself that I wholeheartedly thought were true. What kind of things? Things such as:

I'm not handsome. Nobody will ever want to be with me. No one will want to be with a guy shorter than six feet. I'm

brown skin and not light skin, that's why I'll always be single.
I don't have six pack abs, so no one will find me attractive.

All these things I said to myself and over and over again I would repeat them. Do you do this, too? What are the things you say to yourself over and over again? Do you realize the house of lies you build in doing so? Isn't it crazy how by saying these things over and over again it becomes the reality of our lives?

One day as it often happens, I re-read a verse in the Bible that said, "The power of life or death is in the tongue" and while I've read this many times, on this occasion, it really struck me. I started to think, what if I stopped repeating things that I did not want in my life? What if instead of telling these lies that were not serving me, I began to say some positive lies? I know what you're thinking, lying is not good at all, how can it be positive, but follow me.

What are affirmations? These are things you are speaking over and over to yourself that are positive and empowering, right? Are you really those things at the moment? Nope. These are "positive lies" and just like the negative lies, saying them over and over again eventually become your truth. With that being said, I want to issue you a challenge to tell positive lies to yourself for the next twenty-eight days. Spend the next four weeks speaking positive lies to yourself. You will see how your life will begin to reflect what you speak over time. Speak into existence the life you desire and not the one you wish to never live.

GEM #30

What was meant to break you is often the thing that makes you.

"N-now th-that, that don't kill me

Can only make me stronger

I need you to hurry up now

Cause I can't wait much longer"

Remember those lyrics from the song, "Stronger" by Kanye West. That jam definitely helps me kick my workout into another gear anytime it comes on. It gives me a kick in the butt when I feel like the thing that I'm going through is killing me. It reminds me, though, how much stronger I'm getting as a result of it, too.

When I think about this song, I cannot help but think about the story of Job in the Bible. I think about how much he suffered, losing his possessions, losing family member after family member, getting sick, if something bad could happen to a person, it all happened to him. The first part of his story, of being broken and going through suffering, would cause the average person to easily check out, but in doing so, you miss how the story ends Job receives a double portion of blessings!

This gem is to help you when you are in a season of despair. When you feel like you're getting doors shut in your face time and time again and are at the brink of losing all hope. That is where this gem can bring you comfort in knowing that in the breaking there is a blessing.

A great illustration of this is what happens when we workout. When you are doing your squats, bicep curls, pushups, lunges, your muscle fibers are being torn apart. You are literally ripping your muscle fibers, breaking them down, but what happens next? They repair themselves and get STRONGER as a result. Without the breaking, there is no repairing themselves and there is no getting stronger. Many times we are not able to level up in life because we leave at the breaking stage, not realizing that it's a part of the making stage, too. The thing that is breaking you down is not here for your demise, it's a stimulus to help you rise to a bigger, stronger, faster, better version of yourself.

Think back to a moment where you thought you could not go any further and then you did—how did that feel? That was a moment of making for you. The tough part about this whole thing, though, is in the moment we do not realize what it is because the pain can be tough to bear. That is when we have to keep faith like Job did and trust that all things work out for our good. Instead of thinking you're falling apart, think about how things are falling into place. The next time you find yourself in a stage of breaking, smile and when people ask you why you're smiling in the midst of everything falling apart around you, share how they aren't falling apart, they're falling in place. The peace that surpasses all understanding, let it be your refuge in those moments so that your stronger self will not be denied. There is a stronger, better version of you waiting to come out, do not forfeit that blessing because of the breaking, that is where the blessing lies.

GEM #31

What we can do together trumps what we can do apart.

ME, MYSELF, AND I.

Is this the players on your team?

If you're like me, there is one person you trust more than anyone else, and that's ME! I don't like putting my destiny in the hands of others and chances are you don't like to either. Perhaps this mindset came from doing class projects in school where you got a grade you did not like because the other members of the group did not carry their weight. Or maybe it was having to do all the work myself anyway, so who needs the other members? Maybe it's the band group syndrome of seeing one artist being more talented than the others. Although there are "perceived" benefits to just being an army of one, how far can one really go alone?

There's a quote that says, "If you want to go fast, go alone, if you want to go far, go with others." How far do you want to go? Do you want to be a one hit wonder, or do you want to build a legacy that lasts a lifetime? If you are looking to do anything big—and I know you are because you would not be reading this book—then you have to build a team. A team does not need to be a fifty person company, but it cannot be a team of Me, Myself and I. The larger the impact, the more troops are needed for the mission.

What are you looking to do? Knowing you, I bet your answer is to lead a life that impacts others. My question is, who is on your team to ensure that happens? Together more can be done than a team of one. For you who is reading this, know that I am on your team. At the same time, we need more troops.

Now I know what you might be saying. You tried trusting people in the past and they messed up your dreams, they crapped on your visions. I get being burned and not wanting that to happen again, but the mission is too big for us to handle on our own. I myself have been burned by building a team and seeing it fall apart and it's allowed me to trust only myself, but I repeat again, the calling, the mission, is too big for one person to handle alone. Speed is not the name of the game here, distance is, and, in a marathon, I need to have others around me and so do you.

Where can you find other team members? Meet-up groups with people who are like minded, going on Eventbrite to social events, and joining Facebook groups filled with people who have similar goals, are all ways to find team members.

Let's get together and achieve more as the acronym T.E.A.M. reminds us:

Together

Everyone

Achieves

More

GEM #32

Help someone who can do nothing for you.

I LOVE HELPING PEOPLE, but more so, when they can do something for me. This kind of help is a little tainted, though. The purest form of help is what this gem says, helping someone who can do nothing for you. Scratching the back of someone, not because you want them to scratch your back, but because it's the right thing to do or it's the loving thing to do. I think about how Jesus died for us without any guarantee that we would love him back.

What would it look like if we were doing things on that level? How would it transform us? How would the world look if we were all just givers? It's said that the greatest leaders are the greatest servants. This gem is a call for leadership. It's to see you rise to become the head and set the example. If the world is to right its course, someone has to take the lead and show us how, so why not you? I know this is not an easy thing to ask for, we cannot help but want someone to reciprocate the kind gestures we've done, but will we stop at doing our best if that gesture is not returned? What about helping for helping sake and not for a reward. The mere act of helping someone is reward enough. When holding a door for the elderly, a thank you would be nice, but it's not a pre-requisite for me to do so.

If the world applies this gem, the world will never lack anything. We will live in a world of abundant love, abundant grace, and abundant mercy. It starts with you and I storing this gem in our hearts to make that happen, will you join me in the challenge of doing so?

GEM #33

Wisdom is not meant to be kept, but shared

IMAGINE THE FOLLOWING SCENARIO...

A doctor works diligently trying to find a cure for cancer and finally does so. After finding the cure, he locks the protocol for the cure in a vault, never sharing it with others.

What a jerk, right? Can I confess to you for a moment? There have been times I've been that jerk. No I do not have the cure for cancer, but there is information that I've received which I've not shared with people in the past and consider this my moment of clarity where I see that my mindset toward information was all wrong.

This mindset is rooted in what is called scarcity. People do not like to share what they know because they believe if more people know there is less for them to have. The reality, though, is the opposite. The more you go ahead and share, the more we get. It reminds me of the song, "What's Mine Is Yours" from All Dogs Go to Heaven that says, "The more you share, the more you're gonna get."

Wisdom is not something meant to be put in a closet for no one to use, it is designed to help transform lives and that can only happen when it's accessible to us all.

I remember many times speaking with a client of mine sharing my secrets and how by sharing, my client would share something back that would make the secrets ten times more valuable. That would not have been possible, though, if I stayed in a scarcity mindset and kept that information to myself.

Our motto should be "always give" and then when you've given, "give some more." Isn't that what God does? He does not hold back his blessings, He gives us more than we can even comprehend, despite the fact that we deserve none of it. Let us model after him with how we share wisdom.

GEM #34

The key to a healthy decision is weighing the costs of now and later

WHEN IT COMES TO healthy decision making, we are often prisoners of the moment. We focus on what's good for me right now, missing the fact that our later is connected to it. Similar to a previous gem, but this comes with a more practical step for us to consider. If you're going to make the healthiest decision you must be mindful of the present, as well as the future and the connection between the two. When it comes to processing your decision, you don't only want to think about the pros and the cons for right now, but you also want to think about the pros and the cons for later as well.

What does that look like? Let us think about it from a financial standpoint. There is something you want to get right now, not something you need, but something you want, but your checking account does not have that money, but you do have it in your savings or 401k account. You can go and get it right now, but what impact will that have on your future? Will you have to pay a penalty for removing the money? What about if you have a great NEED in the future but because you made your decision in a vacuum, you sabotage your future because of you wanting to get something right now?

Many times I've seen people cut themselves off from future success because they were prisoners of the moment. They did not count the costs of now and later; instead, they made decisions in an unhealthy, unwise way. By no means am I telling you to analyze everything you do to the point that you do nothing at all. I'm just simply saying that it's wise and healthy when making decisions to realize what you do right now connects to the later you will experience and the peace comes from knowing that you made a decision that is good for now and good for later whenever possible. There are exceptions to every rule, but this one more times than not, will help you have less anxiety.

What decisions do you have coming up? What are the

pros and cons of that decision today? What are the pros and cons of that decision tomorrow? How do you feel about the decision after evaluating the pros and cons of both the present and future? If you are at peace with it, go forward with the decision, if you are not at peace with it or willing to take on the cons that come with it, don't do it. It's simple—that does not mean easy— but it's definitely not impossible. You can begin making wise healthy decisions today by implementing this gem in your life.

GEM #35

Being over prepared, prepares you for the unexpected.

Winners win.

Have you ever heard this phrase before?

Have you ever met someone like this before?

Someone who no matter what is happening to them always finds a way? What if I told you that was not an accident, but it was by design? What if I told you that you too can create that in your own life, would you be interested?

The secret to living out the DJ Khaled, "All I Do Is Win" is being over-prepared. In life, you will have many unexpected things happen to you, but those who prepare more are the ones best suited to handle the weird bounces that life brings.

Whenever I think about this gem, I remember a video of Steph Curry practicing. In the video, I see Steph catching basketball passes that are less than ideal, these are outright bad passes, but he is practicing how to perform even in those conditions. Then, I go ahead and watch a game and see the unlucky bounce, the bad pass and still he finds a way to sink the shot or make the right play. How is that so? It's because he over-prepared. He's proactive in his approach, so he positions himself to win.

Winners win because they do what losers are unwilling to do. Winners win because while it's sunny, they fix the roof. Winners win because they don't just prepare for ideal, they even practice the less than ideal situations.

You are a winner when you download this approach in your preparation. Do not just prepare for what is being asked, prepare for a little bit more. This way when life brings you some pop quizzes you won't be caught off guard. I mention this is my first book, The Thirst Is Real, how we hate pop quizzes because we did not see them coming. Imagine if you came ready for the justin-case a quiz? While everyone else sweats, you got that song, "I Ain't Worried About Nothin" playing in your head because you were MORE THAN READY.

I want you to win more and in order for you to win like never before. Your preparation will need to be like never before, too. Always put in 110 percent. Put more than what is required so that your compensation can also be more than. It's the secret winners use to always win, and now you have it as well.

GEM #36

If you pray only when you have a problem, then you have a problem.

IF YOU STAY READY, you don't have to get ready. This statement comes to mind when I think about prayer. Many times we use prayer as a last resort when it should be our first resort. Don't tell me I am the only one that prays when things are falling apart and forget to do so when things are together. This is a problem.

Prayer should not be something we do when something is wrong, it should be something we do to ensure things STAY right.

At the time of writing this, I'm reminded of the verse that says, "Apart from God we can do nothing" and how much I've tried to do things apart from God because I don't consistently pray. MC Hammer had a song that says, "You have to pray just to make it today." Do you want to make it today? I can promise you won't make it long term without applying what this gem says.

Prayer is the ultimate security blanket. How so? Because it provides a double whammy. It provides insurance and assurance—HELLO!

In the book *The 7 Habits of Highly Effective People*, by Stephen Covey, the first habit he talks about is being proactive. Being proactive is praying even when you don't have a problem. What if praying actually kept distance between you and the problem? You'd never know if you don't do it again and again. I believe that prayer has kept us from problems that could have knocked us out. It's why the Holy Spirit interceding on our behalf is so awesome because there are many times we are not even aware of the danger we are about to get into. With that in mind, position yourself to be insured and assured by using the power of prayer all the time and not only when something is wrong.

GEM #37

Before you can score, you must first have a goal.

"If you don't know where you are going, you might end up somewhere else." – Yogi Berra

I ALWAYS LAUGH WHEN I hear someone say we are going on a "joy ride" because of Yogi's quote. By definition, a joy ride is getting in a car and not knowing where you are going. That might be cool when you're kids and end up somewhere else, but as adults we know that time is money and we need to be more intentional about where I'm going.

That is where this gem comes into play. For us to win at the game of life, to arrive at success, we have to define it first. One of the missing links toward achieving success is the fact we have never defined what it is for ourselves. The hustle of life often times makes us skip this necessary step. I, for one, am guilty of this. I hate planning. I hate sitting in my ideas. I'm what you call a hit it and quit it guy when it comes to my ideas. I live for the spark. I'm the microwave guy and not so much the oven or slow cooker guy. And because of this rush to get to where I want to go, I often miss where I really should have been all along.

Maybe you are like me and you too are in a rush? Maybe you're in a rush because you feel you should have already arrived at your destination; but, let this be a reminder to you to SLOW DOWN!

Slow down and establish first what the goal is so that every action thereafter counts FOR you instead of AGAINST you. Doing the work once is hard enough, rushing through it might require you to do it again. If you did not have time the first time, where will you find the time to do it a second time?

Here's how to use this right now. Get a sheet of paper and write down where you want to go. I want you to identify your ideal day. What did you do upon waking up; what did you do for lunch; where are you? Map out all the details, this way the goal is CLEAR! Once the goal is clear to you, you will then be able to know what steps to take to reach it. Until then, you are wasting your best energy and might end up somewhere you never meant to be. As Jeff Yalden, a motivational speaker says, "Take time to think." Establish what your goal is so you can score points toward it in your future.

GEM #38

You can overcome every doubt by letting go of the "but" and holding onto the "do."

Do you know what the number one dream killer is?

Doubt!

Doubt kills more dreams than failure does. Can you believe that? I've seen many people fail and still make their dreams come true, but those who doubt? They never see their dreams come true. You see, failure does not kill dreams; in fact, failure can sometimes be the fuel that makes dreams happen. In order to fail, guess what needs to happen? You have to do something. If you attempted to make something happen and it did not work, that is actually not failure if you learned something from it. The attempt comes with information, feedback that can help you achieve what it is you're looking to accomplish. It helps you achieve your dreams, but with doubt, that does not happen.

When someone has doubt, what do they do? They think about what can happen. They are stuck in the thinking stage, and it is not a bad thing to be there, but to be stuck in it is never good. If you can think about a time you were full of doubt, you probably were thinking about all the reasons you should not do the thing or were coming up with excuses as to why you should not do it yet, possibly. A word people say a lot when they are about to make excuses is the word BUT.

Take for example, a story I heard from one of Dr. Rob. He shared with me a story of a young lady in high school who was the hottest girl in school but when it came time for the prom she had no date. How is it possible the hottest girl in school would have no date to the prom? I'm pretty sure a lot of guys had doubt about her saying yes. I can hear the conversations now.

"I would ask her, **BUT** she would never go for a guy like me".

"**BUT** if I ask her, will she say yes?"

"I would ask her, **BUT** she probably has someone already".

These are just excuses made by us to protect ourselves from failure. When you understand that failure is not the worst thing that happens to you, you will then let go of the "but" and take the "do".

Just in case you have not noticed, both the word "DO" and "BUT" is in the word "DOUBT".

That is how this gem came about. I shared this at a seminar I conducted and the people in the room almost fell out of their chairs when I broke it down. Thank you, God, for that wisdom, because I sure could not have come up with it myself. I remember there was this one girl at the seminar who told me about her dream to be in the film industry, BUT her parents did not think it was a real career choice so there she was stuck living a nightmare instead of living out her dreams.

But I'm glad she applied this gem because I recently read how she is in California now, inching closer to her dreams. This gave me all types of excitement. How did she overcome her doubt? By letting go of the "BUT" and holding onto the "DO."

If there is something you are doubting right now, I promise you that staying on your but(t) won't get you any closer to it. I also promise you that no matter what happens, you will get something from "doing" something. Remember failure is not failure if you learn from it. That is what we call a lesson. Don't lose your opportunities to level up because of doubt. You can make your dreams come true by being true them and doing something about it today!

GEM #39

You get to success road by going through "suc" road first

THIS IS ONE OF my absolute favorites. And it's so hard to accept it but I'm always big on playing with words. As I listened to the word and kept on saying it to myself, this revelation came to me. Sometimes when you hear a word, it's great to say it slow. Say it a different way. You can even have fun with it and say it in different accents if you want. When speaking to an audience I always ask the question of who wants to be successful, to see who I have in the room and never have I found someone who does not want it. We all do. But we've been led to believe that we can skip steps to getting it.

Just because you want it does not mean we get to

choose exactly how we go about getting it. If I told you there were two ways to get success, one where it was easy, smooth, no difficulties and another that was hard, rough, and challenging, which one would you choose? The easier road, right? Who wants to go through hard, rough, and challenging if they do not have to? That is where we fall into the trap that I talked about earlier in regards to the path of least resistance—not realizing that we were meant to grow and that growth often comes when we are challenged. Growth is the goal that opens up the doors to other goals being achieved.

To get to SUCCESS road, you have to be willing to go through those roads that suck. I'm not saying that it will always suck; I'm just saying you have to be willing to go there if necessary to make sure you get to success road. It's said that the fastest way from Point A to Point B is a straight line, but the minute we see an obstacle on that line, we try to find another way, thus making the journey longer than it has to be. If the fastest way is a straight line, then guess what direction you should go in? Straight, even if there is a boulder in the way trying to stop you. Going straight at it is necessary, it's good for you and it's how you will get there.

DO NOT EXPECT SUCCESS to be an easy road to get to because it is not. Do not let social media fool you into believing that it is easy, those are just the highlight reels that everyone is posting. Posting the ugly side of it wouldn't get as many likes so you rarely see those moments of failure—the moments of people wanting to give up. We never see the practice, we just see the game.

If you want to be successful, be willing to go through "suc" road and you will get there a lot faster. This works in any interest area—consulting, teaching, running a business, becoming an actor or actress. It works when you understand it and apply it to your life.

GEM #40

A blessing received before its time is a curse.

THE BISHOP STRIKES AGAIN. This is another gem from Bishop TD Jakes. He shared a story about what it would look like if he gave his son a car because he wanted it. At the time, his son was a little child, but he kept on asking his dad for a car. TD Jakes then explained how if he gave in to his son asking to get the car at that time, it would have been bad for his son because he was not ready for it yet. Getting a car is a blessing, but if it's before it's time, it can be a curse. His decision making is not up to par yet, his brain is not developed yet, heck, he cannot even see over the steering wheel to have a car!

You might want something right now, and you are frustrated with how long it's taking for you to get it. You know that God loves blessing His children and you cannot help but ask if He does not love you as much because you're waiting and waiting and have not received it yet. What if God is withholding your blessing because He knows it's not time for you yet. What if He's preparing you so that when you receive it, you can not only benefit from it but get to thrive because of it.

Think about the many people who have won the lottery. Quite the blessing, right? How come so many get this blessing and then only a few years later are more broke than they were before they acquired their fortune? It's because they received it out of turn. You cannot build on a faulty foundation. What if you are being refined and made into a solid rock before your blessing comes so that it won't tumble over with the slightest breeze? What if right now you are quicksand, and anything that you're given now will only sink into the ground?

This would be devastating, wouldn't it? My heart breaks to see someone receive what they thought was a blessing and then it slips away from them. Instead of being frustrated in the middle of the wait, change your perspective, and realize that you are solidifying the platform for your blessing to stand on. This simple shift will help you appreciate the waiting period and you will cherish the blessing more when it comes. It's coming—best believe it. Great things take time, and what is coming for you is great. Don't settle for good enough, don't settle for just right now, think about how great it will be when you get it at the right time.

GEM #41

Struggle is perfection in progress

ARE YOU BEGINNING TO notice a theme with these gems? "Suc" road, path of least resistance, struggle, hard, these are things that people do not talk about. The idea behind this book is not to give you a fairytale, but to help you create a masterpiece of a year and a masterpiece with your life that will inspire you to do more and inspire those around you to want the same for themselves. This is why these gems are the way they are.

With that being said, let's jump into our next gem: Struggle is perfection in progress. Remember earlier when we talked about "progression over perfection"? Here we are again. I firmly believe that how we view things shapes how we do things. It's why 20/20 Living was born. It was born because I realize that our vision is so important to how we view life. Helen Keller herself talked about how the only thing worse than being blind is having sight without vision. Vision is huge!

If I can help you to see struggle as perfection in progress you will be more excited and more engaged in how you handle your struggles.

Not too long ago, I was working with a client of mine who was writing a book on financial literacy. This book, I believed, would be an amazing gem for those who lack a sound base of financial education. But the process was honestly a struggle. I can recall my client being frustrated with how the process was going in the beginning. It was not going fast enough for him and we were revisiting a lot of things over and over again so I could understand his frustration, but how come I was not frustrated? I was not frustrated because I understood what was happening. We were struggling. I understood that struggle was perfection in progress, so I enjoyed the back and forth. It's frustrating, but it's worth it when you keep on going. When I explained to him this gem, his perspective changed.

That is where change comes, in our perspective. I noticed it with another one of my clients. I remember how frustrating it was for her originally to do videos, but then we talked about it, changed her perspective. I got her loving the struggle of it and before you know it, thirty videos were recorded like a freaking champ. Could you have imagined this happening without the changing her perspective of struggle? Impossible! But when she noticed that every time she did it ,she got better, I saw her smile get brighter. I saw her gaining confidence. That is what happens when someone grows, when someone is progressing.

So remember examples like these every time you find yourself in a struggle. Remember that this is just perfection in progress or as I like to call it, "Your process of perfecting." Every struggle you're willing to face, is a day closer to you experiencing the perfection you desire.

Oh, by the way, that guy and his book? He went on to be featured on Black Enterprise, did a TEDx talk and is off to the races. You, too, will experience that breakthrough sooner than you think when you download this gem into your spirit, your mindset, and live it out.

GEM #42

If you don't stretch your limits, you will set your limits.

I REMEMBER THE TIME I specifically kept on thinking in fixed mindsets. Carol Dweck's work breaks this down so well, it warrants repeating. In her book, she talks about two mindsets, a fixed mindset and a growth mindset. The fixed mindset believes you was born with a certain amount of ability and that it cannot be changed, thus the word fixed. The growth mindset, however, speaks to the idea that through training, things can be developed to become greater. Your ability is not a finite. It's something that can be molded.

This gem speaks to the fact that we have endless potential but how we view our potential and our relationship to developing it, can determine if it has an end or not. I think of the Lamb Chops song that says, "This is the song that never ends, and it goes on and on, my friend, some people started singing it, not knowing what it was, but they continued singing it forever, just because." What if we looked at our potential the same way. What if we said that it never ends, and that it goes on and on, even if you don't understand—let that be the reason to put a period on what it could be. Your potential is the one place where I will accept you having a run-on sentence. Do not put a period on what you can do because you can do more than you imagine or think.

Here's an exercise I want you to do to help program you to take the limits off. I want you to write down three of your wildest dreams. I don't want you to write three wild dreams that are not yours. In order for this to, these have to be things you really want. After you write them down, I want you to ask the question, what would make this idea even larger? How can I make this even bigger? Ask that question two to three times and allow your mind to imagine what could be.

This is how my "Art of Making History Tour" came to be. It started from a friend asking me to come speak at her school during Black History Month and so I did. I then said, "How can I make this even bigger?" The answer to that question was: Build a formal presentation that you can have for Black History Month for years to come. I then said, "How can I make that bigger?" That's when the idea of why should one school get it? Go do a tour and visit multiple campuses, multiple schools. Now it's something I look forward to every February. It all started with just asking the question, "How can I make this even bigger".

What idea that you have right now is waiting for its growth spurt? You can make it bigger. Remember, the quality of our questions determines the quality of our lives. Ask away!

GEM #43

When you act on your commitments instead of your feelings, you'll be unstoppable

When you think of the word unstoppable what comes to mind? I did a google images search for unstoppable and a lot of freight trains appeared. What if you could be like a freight train? No one would want to stand in the way of a freight train, right? What if I could help you become that unstoppable? So unstoppable that when circumstances come, your dreams would not be derailed. Would you like that?

If the answer is yes, which I know it is, then it's time to change the order of operations a little bit. When it comes to those who are unstoppable, the order of operations is always commitments first, feelings second. It's that gem we talked about earlier which said if I wait until I feel it, I may never see it. Unstoppable people always see it, because they don't wait for the feelings to come in order to act.

Think about how many times you've done something that you said you would do because you committed to it. Did you regret it afterward? Most of the time we do not if it is in line with something we want. They say that regrets weighs tons and discipline weighs ounces. I'd rather carry ounces than tons, no matter how strong I am. The disciplined person is unstoppable. The disciplined person is reliable and gets the job done even when the conditions and circumstances are not convenient for them.

I want you to be unstoppable, but there is a cost. The bill will have commitments on it.

What will your commitments be in? A word of caution: Do not have too many commitments. Less is more here. The more commitments you have, the less reliable you will be, and that is not a foundation that breeds unstoppable success.

There is a lion in you that is waiting to break free: it's

waiting on you to define what those commitments are. Do that and you will see how your life will change. You won't even have to worry about telling people what you did because that level of commitment will produce results that are obvious.

It's how I feel about my weight loss journey. I don't have to talk about it; it does the talking for itself. I know self-promotion is something that can be a challenge for you, but when we define our commitments and go at them with everything we have, your results will promote you! Are you ready?

GEM #44

You cannot have a million dollar dream with a minimum wage work ethic.

ERIC THOMAS THE HIP Hop Preacher gets credit for this gem, but this even goes back to the Bible where it talks about reaping what you sow.

Another part of the Bible speaks to whom much is given, much is required, too, which speaks again to the COST of things. You've seen that as an underlying theme with the gems in this book—the work that is involved in getting what we want. Wanting is easy, working is hard. Everyone wants, but not everyone works. Kevin Hart has a quote that says, "Everybody wants to be famous, but not everyone wants to put the work in," This takes me back to the gem #26: "You can have whatever you like if you are willing to pay the price".

We sometimes have a disconnect when it comes to work and dreams because when we think of dreams, they are free. It's like putting stuff on Pinterest, it does not cost me anything to put it on a board, but it does cost me a lot to make that board become something I experience in real life. This gem is simply a reminder to make sure your work matches what you long for. If you want something great, know the price is just as great.

I know you've done some hard work before and have seen the benefits of it. Sometimes we just forget, so this is a reminder of what it can do for our lives.

I leave you with one of the greatest boxers' quote that sums this up perfectly.

"I hated every minute of training, but I, said, 'Don't quit. Suffer now and live the rest of your life as a champion.'" — Muhammad Ali

Let's get 'em, champ!

GEM #45

S.A.F.E. - Suckers Attempt For Excellence

THE GREATER THE RISKS, the greater the rewards.

Can I brag for a moment?

My wife Marsha is excellent. If you know me, you know this to be true because I always broadcast her. I even joke with her that I only get over 100 likes on social media when she is included in the picture!

What does Marsha have to do with this gem? I almost ended up having a life without her. How come? Because I was afraid of taking risks.

At the time, we were really good friends and the last

thing I wanted to do was ruin that by letting her know I liked her and wanted to be more than friends. I quite often think about what if I'd played it "safe" and did not take the risk, what would have happened? I don't stay on that thought for long because I could not imagine my life without her.

When I look back at my life and look at all the things that are excellent, I realize that I got all of them the same way. I got them by not playing it SAFE. I got them because I was willing to risk it all to get it all. Anything else then that is S.A.F.E. (Suckers Attempt For Excellence).

If you desire something less than great, just bypass this gem, it won't make sense to you. I know that is not you, though, because great people want great things, and you are a great person. I share this gem with you because I would hate for your fear or being risk averse to stop you from experiencing excellence in all areas of your life. It's my desire for you to find excellence in your career, excellence in your side hustle, excellence in your friendships, excellence in a relationship, down the road, if you're single. I desire excellence for you and I would not be honest if I did not tell you that in order to get there, you must be willing to take risk.

Years ago, when I joined a speaking course by my mentor and now friend, Arel Moodie, that was a risk. That was an investment of $2,000. Money I honestly did not have. When I joined the mastermind and paid all those thousands of dollars, that was a risk. When I paid to attend a conference with no guarantee of getting booked, that was a risk. But on the other side of taking all those risks, I was able to build a speaking business (not where I want it to be, yet, but nowhere near what it was), I made amazing friends that I get to dream with and impact lives with, too.

All of these excellent things came because I was willing to not play it safe.

What bold and courageous risk have you been hesitant to take? What is something you can do today to move toward making that come true?

I would rather go as close to the line as possible, than to play as far from the line as possible. It's risky, I won't say it's not, but the reward is worth it—no matter how long it takes.

GEM #46

No matter how slow you go, you're still ahead of the person who never moved.

I'M PROUD OF YOU.

Allow me to say that to you and I sincerely mean it. Sometimes it's hard to pursue something when your efforts have never been acknowledged. I see you putting in the work, I see you reading, I see you studying on YouTube learning how to code or sharpen your skills. I see that despite the fact you are not perfect, you are perfecting.

I know this might sound like what a good parent tells a child when they don't want them to quit, but I am saying this to you because I do understand that no matter how slow you go, you are ahead of the person who has never moved. It's because I understand that the hardest part of the journey is often the beginning.

My mentor told me many times that it's the start that stops many of us, not the tough times in the middle or the end. People who run marathons understand this concept very well. I was talking to a friend of mine just the other day who ran a marathon and I told her I wanted to run one. A marathon is 26.2 miles and she told me that you never train past like seventeen to eighteen miles, and I was like, huh? How is that so? And she said because the last eight miles or so is easy and you know you can do it because you already did the eighteen. The hardest part? Just getting out there and running. I know this all too well.

Before the days of running five to six miles, I could not even see myself running one mile without gasping for air and needing an oxygen tank, but today I know I'm able to do five to six miles because I kept showing up and running again and again.

You are like me when it comes to the running. You show up again and again. Your actions aren't perfect, but they sure beat those who specialize in perfect inaction. Perfect inaction equals no progress at all. That's like a blank page on your computer. Heck, you might not realize this but the fact that you got drafts upon drafts of your book is further than those who hope to write a book and have nothing written down. Or the twenty videos on your phone is a lot more than the person who got all the gadgets to do a popping video but never recorded one.

I share this all with you as a gem because I don't want you to overlook the progress that you've made. I want you to know that the struggle you have now is your perfection in progress. You are doing it, even if it's slow. Speed is something that comes later. Each step you take today is building the foundation that will allow you to go faster later. Waste no energy in beating yourself up about not doing more. That is not fair to you and will not stimulate growth. What will? Showing up every day.

Cheers to never stopping.

GEM #47

Practice makes permanent

"Practice makes Perfect".

Sorry to burst your bubble, but that is not true. I did not realize that until I heard the great motivational speaker Les Brown speak. When he mentioned this gem of "Practice Makes Permanent," I was like, wow, that is so true. He broke it down to let us know that number one, perfect is not a place we can ever get to and so the quote, while it is nice to hear that we can get to perfect, is not really accurate. However, practice really does help us to develop a habit where we won't need to spend as much energy to do whatever the activity is. It becomes easier as we practice it over and over again.

If you ever wondered, "Will it get easier?" The answer is yes, if you keep on practicing. When you keep on practicing, you will see the level of difficulty decrease as your level of skill increases. They say repetition is the mother of all learning; well, this is what practice does. It helps you learn so that you are able to do more with what you know than before.

With each email you write, with each video you record, with each proposal you submit, with each training you do, you are making those skills permanent. Every action is a drop of water in a cup. Eventually, that cup will get full and then it will overflow. It's how hard becomes easy. Over time.

What things do you struggle at now that you want to get better at? What do you do that takes you far too long and you want to cut the time in half? Whatever those things are, begin to build a consistent practice schedule around it. Even if no one sees it, keep on practicing. I use social media for this purpose. Many people let social media use them, I've decided to make social media work for me by testing out material and seeing what sticks and always practicing on my delivery. This whole thing is a bit of art and also a bit of science and the more practice you put in, the more permanent the skills are, and the more you look like a masterful artist and scientist at the same time.

GEM #48

Only people who do things have haters

LET'S GET SOME HATERS!

I know that sounds weird, but here's why I want haters and why I want you to have them, too. Haters are attracted to doers. Find me anyone who is doing something in their lives, and they are going to have haters. It does not matter if that person is a saint, they will have haters. Haters are now popular. Look at anyone on social media doing something and you will always find someone in the comments with something to say.

Why did this gem make the book? Because I realize that too many of us try to figure out how to do something and not have haters. I have bad news for you. It's not possible. It's not possible for you to not have haters if you are doing something. By nature, haters are people who don't do anything but have something to say about those who do. Anytime I see a hater do something, I always go to their page to see what they are doing and guess what I find? NOTHING! They just like to give commentary, but they are not out there doing the work. This baffles me when I think about how much energy people put out hating on others when, if they just took that energy creating something for themselves, they would be able to win, too.

I share this gem with you because I know sometimes the fear of being judged comes up and might stop you from putting yourself out there. But the reality is that is not a good enough reason for holding back. Haters are proof that you're taking action. If you don't have haters, then you are probably not doing anything worth talking about. Haters don't hate on things that are not worth talking about. Do you see anyone hating on the local chicken spot where you live? Nope. But everyone has something to say about Chick Fil-A, don't they? It's because they are doing the darn thing. No shade on the local chicken spot, by the way.

You also should be doing the darn thing. Instead of being jealous of others, let's begin to create things that others will be jealous of. Use your energy wisely. Spend your time on asset accumulation and not activities that are liabilities. Wondering how to create something that won't have haters, that is a liability activity. That is you wasting time. Remember, we cannot manage time but we sure can spend it. I suggest you spend it on doing things that will attract haters, because that means you are doing something. Let's work to give them something to talk about. Take action so that we can keep the haters alive. Don't waste time trying to figure out how to kill them. And listen, I've been a hater myself, so I know first-hand being jealous. I won't go as far as to write a comment on someone page, but I say it in the confines of my home. But it's a waste of time and I realize that now and hope you do, too. Realize that haters are trophies. They are trophies for those who DO STUFF.

Go get your gold medal; let's get to work.

GEM #49

Old ways won't open new doors.

IF YOU'VE EVER FOUND yourself working on something and feeling like no progress is being made, it might be time to switch things up.

We are almost at the end of the book—can you believe we are at Gem #49? This gem is not a long one but put it in your back pocket as a good reminder. This gem I learned when I was reading a newsletter of a speaker coach that wrote about his business and the struggles he had in growing it. In the newsletter, he shared how he was able to build his business to $100,000, but then his business plateaued and was not able to get any higher than that. He shared how the stuff that was working before simply was not working anymore, so he went to his brother who had a more successful business. His brother asked him what was wrong, and the speaker coach said, "I've been doing the things that got me to scale my business to $100,000, but now I'm trying to get to $250,000 and those things are not working anymore." His brother then said to him, "Well, the old way of doing things, won't open up the new door that you're looking to get into". He told him that in order to get that new goal, it's going to require a new approach. What he had done before was the $100,000 plan, now he needed a $250,000 plan.

You might be thinking what is the $250,000 plan? Why can't he just do 2.5 times what he was doing to get to the $100,000? I was thinking the same thing. I thought it was that simple, but it really is not. These are two different roads completely that require a renewed mind so you can spot the opportunities that people who make $250,000 think about. So the speaker coach began hanging around different people. He understood the earlier gem about how "your company affects your company" so he decided to change the circles he found himself in and started to see his thinking change. He began taking different actions from his new circle and in no-time was able to go ahead and reach the $250,000 goal. he repeated this process again to eventually get to seven figures.

What does this mean for both you and I? Maybe the people we are around, our ride or dies, might be the reason our business, our dreams, are dying. Maybe we need a new way. One of the ways I've discovered is by getting a coach. A coach who has been where you want to go might be able to share with you new ways to do things that you were not aware of.

This gem is scary because we find comfort in the old, but your dreams require you to be uncomfortable in order to experience the new things, so be willing to be uncomfortable.

GEM #50

Would you give yourself a raise or fire yourself based on how you've been working on your dreams?

CALLING ALL CREATIVES!

This gem is an important one that I think is super crucial for those who enjoy doing work that they are passionate about. I've found this to be a struggle for many who are creative and are trying to build a business for themselves. A nine to five job will have these parameters in place for us but rarely are those parameters put in place when we are working on our own stuff.

I was given this gem by one of my mentors who asked me to take an honest look at how I was approaching my business. I guess he was tired of me coming up with the same questions over and over again. He said, "Geo you got a book that is called *The Thirst is Real*, let me ask you a question is your thirst real?" The nerve of my mentor using my words against me. All joking aside, I needed him to say that to me. He told me, "Geo, if you were a boss and had yourself as a worker, would you give yourself a raise or would you fire yourself?"

After that conversation, I began to look at my work for the past week, and the weeks before that, and as I began looking at how I started my mornings and realized that watching *First Take* on ESPN2 had nothing to do with my work; I was taking a vacation and stealing money from the company. You would think I was working more for ESPN than I was working for 20/20 Living. The questions my mentor asked me reminded me that I need to take what I do more seriously and have to find a way to constantly evaluate how I'm performing. This is something you, too, should have for yourself. Do you have a way to rate how you're doing, or do you wait until it's too late to do anything about it? You should always be aware of what the scoreboard says so you can adjust. That is why companies have team meetings. They don't have them just for the hell of it. They have them because they know you cannot fix what you don't measure; you cannot know how to grow if you don't know what is going on.

Do you have a checks and balances system for yourself? If not, please apply this gem as a way on a simple level to rate yourself on how you are doing with your own dreams. Would you fire yourself or give yourself a raise based on the work you've done? If the answer is a raise, do more of what you've been doing. If the answer is that you would fire yourself, put yourself on probation and map out specific steps you will begin to get back in good graces with the boss. This is not about beating yourself up, so please be careful of doing that. It's just so that you are aware of what is happening before it gets away from you. We all could use this in our personal lives to ensure that we maximize our lives the same way companies do. Remember earlier I called you a CEO, let's apply this gem and get started in acting like one.

GEM #51

Ask don't assume.

Solve this puzzle.

When you assume you make an _____ out of you and me? Assumptions is another form of protection sometimes. We assume because we want control or we want to appear as if we know something, but I've found that assuming instead of asking, is not wise and can cost you opportunities. The hall of famer and hockey great Wayne Gretzky had a quote that says, "You miss 100 percent of the shots you never take." How many shots have you missed because you assumed that it would not go in, or you assumed the answer was no, so you did not bother asking? So many of us are afraid to hear the word no that we will assume it and just say it to ourselves.

Repeat after me, "I will not reject myself." Say it again for good measure. When you make the assumption that someone is going to tell you no, we reject ourselves. It's like a basketball player blocking his own shot, eliminating any chance that it will go in.

Do not eliminate your own opportunities. Opportunities don't grow on trees, so we want to capitalize on them, not squander them because of our assumptions. Can you think of a time where your assumptions were wrong? A moment when you thought it would go bad and it turned out to be better than you thought? This happens all the time. Too many times we want to know so much, that we prevent God from surprising us. This is why I rarely go into a speech with 100 percent of the material figured out. I know that if I assume I know everything that is going to happen, that I cut off the surprise shifts and turns that God may want to do in my presentation. We do this too with life. Can you imagine missing out on God's best because you assumed what would happen instead of being open and asking?

Remember the prom story from Dr. Rob? Here's the continuation of that story. All the guys assumed she already had a date, so none of them asked. Smh! This is a good reminder of what not asking will bring you. Assume nothing; ask about everything. You will ensure that you do not miss out on possibly the hottest thing that could ever happen to you.

GEM #52

Act the part now and you'll get the part later.

A FEW YEARS AGO, a good friend of mine shared with me that she wanted to purchase a car. This was going to be her first car ever and she was excited to get it. Do you remember ever wanting something that you were excited to get? Do you remember what it took to get it, if you got it? What about something you were excited to get but never got? In the case of my friend, she was able to get a car and since then has been able to get another one and it all came from a simple strategy that I shared with her. It was this gem of "act the part now and you'll get the part later."

I asked her what she needed to do to get the car. She

said she would get a car note and make monthly payments. I instructed her to act as if she had the car right now and she begin to put the car payments into a separate bank account—act the part now. This ties to the gem earlier in the book about preparation being a public display to the thing you want. So month after month, my friend went ahead and made her payments to her account faithfully and then I got that text: "Geo, I got a new car!" She was so happy that she named it "Ruby." She was able to not only get the car but be at peace about it because all along she was preparing herself for this moment.

What moment are looking forward to that you could start acting the part now? Is it a speech? A training in front of a Fortune 500 company? What can you do to act the part now? Maybe it's the outfit you would wear, maybe it's the details of the presentation you would give? Whatever it is, do not wait for the part to act like you got it. Act like you got the part now, and the part you desire will come, and even better, you'll be ready for it! The worst thing that can happen is your opportunity comes and you are not ready for it.

This entire book was not just about you making the next fifty-two weeks a masterpiece, but to help you shape your mind to have the Midas Touch to create whatever you want and to build on that for a lifetime. A great tower is a combination of a bunch of pieces put together well and stack up on top of one another. You, my friend, are a great tower, so let's stack these gems on top of one another and let your success shine the beacon of hope that will provide the rays of sunshine that others can be inspired by.

CONCLUSION

WE HAVE OFFICIALLY ARRIVED at the end of this book. While we are at the end of this book, this is just your beginning.

You now have the thoughts, and now it's time to get the things. The road is clear and it's yours for the taking. I'd love to hear which gem was your favorite, so please shoot me an email at geo@geospeaks.com or hit me up on social media. I agonized over this book, but for good reason. *You.* You are the reason why I worked to get this book written and I'm proud of what you are holding in your hand and will be prouder to see what your hands will hold in the future as a result of what you've read.

Until the next book, this is Geo Derice signing off. I love you and thank you very much for letting me guide you on the journey toward creating a masterpiece out of your life.

ACKNOWLEDGEMENTS

I FIRST WANT TO thank God. I am thankful to my Mom and Dad who unconditional love and prayers are felt everyday. I walk in favor because of their petitions and endless pleas for God's favor. Then are my brothers, Mikey and David. I thank you guys for always believing in my crazy ideas and your full support. To My wife Marsha who at the time of me writing this was burning our kitchen down (just kidding). Thank you for believing in me babe. Thank you for giving me space to be creative, take educated guesses with my business and never lowering your love or faith in me. I am forever grateful to you. To my best friends, my brothers from another mother, Carl, Cleveland, Victor, Gritz, Mackenzie, CJ, Arnel, and Steve thank you for lending me your ears and always encouraging me to keep pushing and blaze new trails. To my sisters from another mother, Tina, Sammetra, Tracey, Jenn Daniel, Peta-Gaye, Lacey, and Candace. I love you guys and am thankful for your encouragement. Also wanted to shoutout my Godparents, Uncle Joey and Aunt Kettly.

Again I could state so many names as I've been blessed with a huge family of supporters such as cousins, uncles, aunts, and friends. I would like to also take a moment to thank my mentors Paul Reddick, Ryan Lee, Arel Moodie, Dr. Rob Gilbert, Genice Reid, Odell Bizzell, and my pastor Brandon Watts who have helped shaped my business mind and help me mature in the later years of my life. Thank you for showing me what is indeed possible. To my colleagues who brave the entrepreneurial trail with me Jessica, Rockell, Malla, thank you for your friendship. To my coaching clients / business friends which are too many to name, thank you for believing in me. Shoutout to you Rahkim Sabree, Andrea Ashcraft, Patrick Pierre Louis, Matt Lebris, Josue Quinones just to name a few.

Lastly, this book would not be what it is without my editor Jessica G, my book cover designer Tri, Justin Reid who shout the cover photo and Chris Derrick my interior book designer. Thanks for helping me get this book to be exactly how I envisioned it.

ABOUT THE AUTHOR

GEO DERICE IS AN international speaker, best selling author, entrepreneur and founder of the company 20/20 Living Inc. He's been featured on Huffington Post, News One, ABC and BET to name a few.

His inspirational messages, engaging and funny stories have helped so many make their dreams a reality. He is also the founder of a publishing company where he consults with future authors helping them become authors. His company in the last three years has helped published 48 books.

Before creating his own company he worked with several million-dollar enterprises specializes in marketing and project management. He was born and raised in Brooklyn, NY and when he's not working can be found watching house hunters with his wife, who he still can't believe married him.

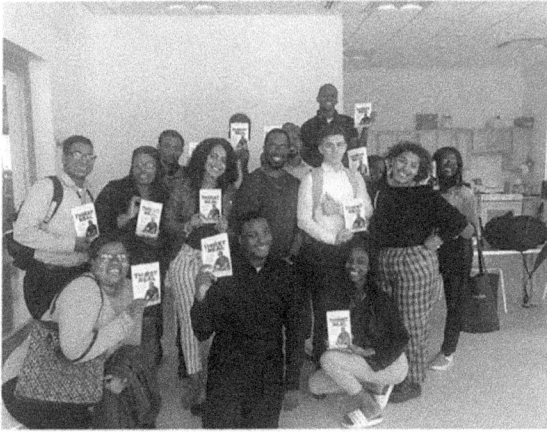

Interested in having Geo come speak at your school or university? Visit www.geospeaks.com or send an email to geo@geospeaks.com

P.S. – Send your picture with this book and receive a surprise gift from Geo himself!